HOPE
&
HEALING

WORDS FROM THE CLERGY
OF A SOUTHERN CITY

GUILD BINDERY PRESS, INC.
MEMPHIS, TENNESSEE

HOPE
AND
HEALING

WORDS FROM THE CLERGY
OF A SOUTHERN CITY

EDITED BY
G. SCOTT MORRIS, M.D., M.DIV.

Copyright © 1995 by
The Church Health Center of Memphis, Inc.

PUBLISHED IN MEMPHIS, TENNESSEE
By GUILD BINDERY PRESS, INC.

Library of Congress Cataloging-in-Publication Data

Editor: G. Scott Morris
Publisher: Randall Bedwell
Managing Editor: Robbin Brent
Layout: Toby Lyon
Cover Art Design: Pat Patterson, Patterson Design Works

CIP

Hope And Healing: Words From the Clergy of a Southern City
p.   cm.

ISBN # 1-55793-055-4
Religious / Inspirational

Printed in the United States of America

1 2 3 4 5 6 7 8 9 10
First Edition

ACKNOWLEDGMENTS

This book is a project of the Church Health Center, which seeks to unite faith congregations in a ministry to the body as well as the spirit. It was supported financially by a generous gift from Baptist Memorial Hospital in Memphis, Tennessee. While many people played a role in its development, I would like to thank the following for their specific tasks:

Helen Shute and Veronica Jackson were superb organizers of the manuscripts, and they helped to keep the pressure on the contributors to meet our deadlines. Andrea Dancy assisted with proofreading the sermons, kept us on track with our publication plans and offered keen insight at strategic decision making points. Lorrie Jackson diligently edited the sermons and assisted with the promotion of the book. Debby DuBois of the <u>Memphis HealthCare News</u> gave us invaluable assistance in writing the back cover. Judy Jackson's editorial guidance helped ensure accuracy and professionalism in the text. Randall Bedwell, our publisher, advised us along the way and provided encouragement when we needed it most. Jean Campbell kept the ship afloat while I was worrying about this book. In addition, I am most grateful to the diverse group of contributing pastors and their staffs who trusted me that the book would be done in a quality form. And finally, I continue to be appreciative of the staff, volunteers, Board members and supporters of the Church Health Center whose faithful work has made a difference in the lives of thousands of people in the name of the Church.

Scott Morris

INTRODUCTION

Hope and healing are both central issues in the life of faith. Hope is at the core of all religious peoples' pursuit of the moral and just life. It is hope that keeps us striving through both the mundane and the sacred experiences of life. Hope is also at the center of our physical existence. In times of both health and sickness, hope can play a dominant role.

This role for hope is often expressed as a desire for healing. But what exactly do we mean by healing? In today's world, do we look for a paralyzed man to take up his pallet and walk? Or do we see healing in more spiritual terms? Is healing the consequence of God working through doctors and science? The questions are many because we do not have a unified view of what healing is. This is especially true among people of faith.

I have found that most people who have strong religious beliefs want to think that God plays a role in matters of sickness and health, but we seldom agree on what that role is. Some believe strongly that God works out a divine plan in which our sickness and suffering are a part. Others will have none of this view and think God's role is only to inspire the miracles of science that are brought about by the men and women who care for our bodies when they are ill. Although rarely stated today, some still argue that all sickness is due to sin, while others insist that sickness is random and God abhors it. This argument has been revisited in the debate around AIDS, and both views are presented in this book.

Healing is an immensely important idea for both Christians

and Jews. There is no debate as to whether or not God wills for us all a healthy existence that affords us the ability to serve God and to be of service to others. But when our bodies fail us, there is great difference of opinion over what role God plays in both our sickness and our return to health. More so, the debate is wide ranging over what to believe when healing does not occur, but instead, one suffers and dies.

Our religious faith is constantly challenged to find expressions that comfort us in times of sickness, suffering and death. We seek hope in the midst of despair caused by illness and brokenness. When at our weakest, we turn to our faith to find such hope for the healing of our many wounds. In trying to offer this comfort, congregations listen to the pastor who speaks for the community and the tradition on these matters. In Christian and Jewish congregations, words of insight and comfort come in the form of a sermon.

This book is a collection of sermons preached by members of the clergy in Memphis, Tennessee, on the subject of healing. The individuals were chosen in an attempt to represent the religious thinking of a moderately-sized city on the role of healing in the life of faith. Members of most major denominations in the city are included, and an attempt was made to reflect both large and small congregations. Young pastors, associate pastors and retired pastors are contributors, along with Bishops and well-known clergy of large, influential churches.

Some pastors were a little reluctant to have their words recorded in a book. Not because they were worried about being held up to public scrutiny, but because of the nature of sermons. Sermons are meant to be heard and not read. They are a spoken art form and are often never written down. Some preachers insist they have never preached the same sermon twice. As hard as that is to believe, it fits with the view that a sermon is for a moment in time, preached to a particular congregation. A written sermon also loses the inflections of the preacher. The pregnant pause at just the right moment is missed. The hand gestures can only be suspected, and the sighs or Amens from the congregation must be imagined.

Despite these weaknesses that result from putting a sermon

in written form, I believe that this collection of sermons has accomplished its task. Together they represent a very diverse array of thought on the nature of God's role in sickness and in health for our bodies, our spirits and our society.

The views presented are not a coherent whole. At times one sermon almost contradicts another. One views healing in only its spiritual form; another seeks to understand how God empowers the surgeon to perform a complex medical procedure. Throughout them all, however, is a running theme that sees God as actively involved and concerned with the lives of individuals who suffer and face despair. God is never blamed for our mortality or lack of understanding. On the contrary, in each sermon it is hope in God's compassion and faith that God suffers with us that unite each pastor's thoughts.

It is my desire that this book will be read by those who themselves are experiencing the need for healing in spirit or body. It is meant to be a source of comfort for us all as we struggle to understand the trials of life.

What also unites each pastor and his or her congregation in this book is support of the Church Health Center, located in Midtown Memphis. This is a ministry of healing that calls on people of faith to unite in an effort to reclaim the church's biblical and historical commitment to care for the body and the spirit of the poor. Congregations from throughout Memphis now support this ministry that provides primary health care for the working poor and homeless. This book is an attempt to put into words what faith has already put into action through the Church Health Center. **(More information about the Church Health Center can be found in the Epilogue.)**

While the tendency will be to turn and read the sermon of the pastor you know best, I am certain you will find revealing insight into hope and healing from the sermon of a pastor you do not know or thought you did not like. That is part of how the mystery of faith and healing works. When we least expect it, God steps forward and gives us a gift that totally surprises us. If you read these sermons with an open mind, the same surprising revelation may happen to you again.

TABLE OF CONTENTS

HEALING IS A BEAUTIFUL WORD

Text: Matthew 9:20–22   William R. Bouknight, III

There was a seminary professor who asked his class one day if anyone could explain the problem of good and evil in the world. "If anyone can explain it," he said, "just raise your hand." John had been dozing, but he awoke just in time to hear the professor ask students to raise their hands. Up went John's hand.

"Oh, this is wonderful," said the professor. "John knows the answer to the problem of good and evil. Please tell us the answer."

John, in considerable embarrassment, replied, "Sir, I did know the answer, but I have forgotten it."

The professor responded with majestic sarcasm, "Class, this is a tragic moment. Only two persons in history have ever understood the problem of good and evil — God and John, and John has forgotten it."

The mystery of healing is in some ways as baffling as the problem of good and evil. For that very reason, many people have totally separated their faith from healing. They believe that the only healing available comes through the physician and the pharmacy. Deep in their hearts they regard prayers for healing as nothing more than wishful thinking. One reason people think this way is that they have been turned off by so-called faith healers on TV. Often they have concluded that these persons were either egocentric showmen or greedy manipulators, and sometimes their suspicions have been correct.

Having said all that, I must remind you that Jesus was continuously involved in a healing ministry and ordered his followers to do likewise. In our scripture lesson, we have miracle stacked onto miracle: four healing miracles in 16 verses. Matthew tells us that Jesus went from village to village "healing every disease and infirmity." In the Gospel of Mark, half of the first eight chapters relate to miraculous healings. When Jesus sent 70 disciples out two by two on a sort of lay witness mission, he commanded them to preach and heal. The Book of Acts records numerous miraculous healings in the early church.

Now, let me add this important fact. The Greek word for salvation (soteria) is also the word for health and wholeness. When Jesus talked about salvation, he meant good physical, emotional, and spiritual health on earth as well as eternal life in heaven. Jesus treated the whole person. Jesus is concerned about your bad back and migraine headaches just as surely as he cares about your moral and spiritual health.

Bishop Roy Nichols watched a baseball game one day. He noticed that just before the pitcher delivered the ball, he lowered his head for just a moment to ask the Lord's help. Just then, the batter stepped out of the batter's box and lowered his head a moment; he too was asking God's help. Just then, the pitcher bowed his head a second time and said, "Lord, please don't take sides. Just watch the game."

While our Lord may be impartial about baseball games, he is never neutral about his people. He is never distant or uncaring. Our God is no absentee Landlord.

My purpose in this sermon is to help us believe that God is a healer. God heals in many ways: through dedicated physicians, through God-given drugs, through trained counselors, and through miracles of faith.

In our scripture lesson, Jesus was on the way to the home of a ruler in order to heal his daughter. Jesus and a large crowd walked along the dusty road. An unknown woman slipped up behind him inconspicuously and just touched the fringe of his robe. Instantly, she was healed.

This woman had suffered from internal bleeding for 12 years. In the first-century Jewish world, this condition made the woman a virtual recluse. She was forbidden to enter the Temple because she was ceremonially unclean. Furthermore, she was not supposed to have close contact with other people. In fact, she wasn't supposed to be in that crowd on the day she was healed.

This poor woman said to herself, "If I can only touch the hem of his garment I will be healed." That, my friends, is faith. The Bible says faith is required for miracles to happen. When Jesus was in his hometown of Nazareth, he could not heal many folks because faith was lacking. This woman had faith, but only a little bit. She didn't have enough to walk boldly up to Jesus and declare her need. She had just enough to reach out inconspicuously and touch his garment. Then, if nothing happened, no one would even know what she had done.

The Bible says that while faith is essential for healing, the amount of faith is not important. If your faith is as big as a tiny mustard seed, Jesus said, it can move mountains.

Woe be to that faith healer on TV or anyone else who says to someone, "You could have been healed, but your faith wasn't great enough." That is a cruel lie. The Bible says faith is essential, but the amount of faith is immaterial. Faith switches on the power for healing. But the power itself is Christ, not our faith.

Then there is that beautiful phrase in the scripture, "Jesus turned and saw her." For a few moments it was as though no crowd existed ... just two persons in the whole world: Jesus and this woman.

When you reach out to Christ in faith, he treats you so personally and powerfully that it is as though you are God's only child on earth. There is no rush, no need to look up your file, no need for small talk. He knows who you are.

Someone has said that if you want to know what an identity crisis is, just try to cash a personal check out of town. But one never has an identity crisis when dealing with Jesus. He confirms your identity. He knows more about you than you do. He made you. And he loves you fervently.

Finally, let me make two statements about healing. First, I think that every believer who asks in faith receives healing. Some are healed with the help of a physician or surgeon. Some are healed through counseling. Some are healed by experiencing forgiveness. Some are healed instantly; some are healed gradually; and some are healed on the way to Heaven. For some people the affliction is physical, like cancer or diabetes. Other people are afflicted emotionally, perhaps because of mistreatment as children. Other people have sick relationships. All of us are afflicted by sin. The single greatest healing miracle on earth happens when an egocentric sinner receives a heart transplant through trust in Jesus Christ as Savior and Lord.

In all honesty, one must admit that some illnesses are more resistant to healings here on earth than others. Father Francis McNutt, the famed Catholic authority on healing, estimates that about half of those he prays for who have physical illnesses are healed or noticeably improved. Of those he prays for who have emotional or spiritual illnesses, 75 percent are healed or noticeably improved. It has been estimated that only about one percent of those persons who come to the famous healing shrine at Lourdes, France, are actually healed. Especially difficult in terms of instantaneous cures are those life-threatening illnesses like cancer and heart disease. Frankly, instant cures for these diseases are quite rare. But a cure will surely come for the believer who asks in faith. If it doesn't happen instantly or gradually, it will surely happen on a person's way to Heaven.

My second statement is this: we are dealing with a mystery that cannot be systematized.

The late Kathryn Kuhlman, one of the most inspired persons ever in the healing ministry, said this:

> I've never written a book about healing even though I've been besieged by requests to do so; simply because I don't know the how and why of healing. I'm still learning the mysterious ways in which God moves. I used to believe that it was always God's will for everybody to be healed here on earth. Now I see that we can't demand or command that God do anything. In general, I still believe that it is God's will to heal. But I can't say absolutely what is or is not his will in a particular situation.

We are dealing with an awesome mystery. When our son Aaron became sick in December 1982, hundreds of people prayed fervently for his physical, instantaneous healing. That prayer was not answered affirmatively. He was healed, I know, on May 27, 1983, on his way to Heaven. Why did God choose to do it that way? I don't know. God was not absent. I have written down a list of 15 specific ways in which God blessed us as we lived through the six-month nightmare of his illness. But God did not heal in the manner I yearned for most. I won't understand that mystery until I walk through Heaven's doors. On this side of glory I just have to trust God. I know his character because I have seen it in Jesus. One day, when I get home, I'll understand. But just because in one very important instance healing was not given in the manner I wanted it, that does not mean that I will doubt God's ability to heal or stop asking for his healing power.

So, we see through a glass darkly in this life, but one day we will understand God even as we are understood by him. But just because we don't understand everything, let's not fail to ask in faith. Let us remember this precious invitation from St. Paul: "In everything by prayer and supplication with thanksgiving, let your requests be made known to God. And the peace of God, which passes all understanding, will keep your hearts and minds in Christ Jesus" (Philipians 4:6, 7).

In 1814, the future of Europe hung in the balance. The British Army under Lord Wellington met Napoleon's French legions at Waterloo. On the day after the battle, the results were flashed by signals across the English Channel. Then the news was passed inland by signal flags flown from towers of cathedrals. From cathedral to cathedral the word went forth. After Winchester Cathedral received the report, a man in the tower began sending the message: "Wellington defeated." Then a fog descended, and nothing else could be seen. Throughout London there was despair and fear. The word spread like wildfire, "Wellington has been defeated at Waterloo." But later the fog lifted, and the complete message could be read. It said: "Wellington defeated the enemy."

Because of some affliction, whether physical, mental, spiritual or relational, a fog may have descended in your life. All the signals may indicate despair and defeat. But if you ask Jesus in simple faith to heal you or someone you love, then one day the fog will lift and health will be restored. It could happen instantly. It might happen gradually. It might happen on the way to Heaven. But one day, the fog will lift. The message will go forth — Jesus Christ has defeated the enemy. He has healed every affliction. The pain is over. The heartbreak has passed. Jesus Christ is Lord.

WHEN GOD SAYS NOTHING

Text: Matthew 15:21–28   Alvin O'Neal Jackson

*I*t is clear from even a casual reading of this text that this is a pathetic episode. A woman torn by worry, gripped and ragged with anxiety, pleading in behalf of her daughter. She says to Jesus, "Have mercy on me." Though it is her daughter who is at home critically ill, she says, "Have mercy on me." This woman is suffering intensely because of her daughter's sickness.

There is nothing more agonizing to a parent than to see his or her child in pain. Any father or mother would rather be stricken himself or herself than to see the child suffer. Any loving parent would rather die than lose a child. I sat recently with a heartbroken father whose son had been brutally murdered, and I heard him say, "I wish I could exchange places with my boy." When John Fitzgerald Kennedy was slain in Dallas in 1963, the elder and now late Adlai Stevenson said, "I wish they had killed me and spared this young man to do the nation's work." This is how the woman in the text felt about the illness of her daughter. She said within her soul, "It should have been me who was stricken. Lord Jesus, Son of David, have mercy on me for my baby, my child, my daughter, the joy of my life is critically and terminally ill ... at death's door."

Alvin O'Neal Jackson

THE MORE LOVE, THE MORE PAIN

The pain of the daughter was tremendous, but the anxiety of the mother was greater still. For the suffering that comes from seeing someone else in pain is almost unbearable, and it increases in proportion to the depth of the love felt toward the person who is sick. Relatives and friends who live with the sick, and wait on the sick hand and foot, day and night, stand more in need of prayer in many ways than the person who is actually ill. The vicarious suffering of the attendant is just as hard to bear, if not harder, as the pain felt directly by the patient. It's a terrible drain on your physical energy. It's a severe strain on your nervous system to see every day somebody you love incurably sick, and there is nothing you can do to reverse it. You can't even relieve it. Sometimes, you can't even make them comfortable. If you take them out of bed, they can't stay long. If you put them back in bed, they just turn and toss. If you put them in a chair, they soon get tired. If you put them back in bed, they are no better. You turn them on the right side, but it brings no relief. You turn them on the left side, but they feel no better. You prepare them a meal, but they can't eat it. You take them liquids, but they can't drink. You give them pills, but it does no good. You send for the doctor, but there is nothing he can do. And the suffering and anxiety of those who live with the sick and work for the sick and wait on the sick is so deep and so serious that they need a double portion of our prayers and God's grace. The more love, the more pain. The more you love, the more you will suffer on the inside. The greatest sufferer on earth is the greatest lover. And that is none other than Jesus the Christ.

He feels our pain. He shares our sorrows. He bears all our anguish and our trouble. "Surely He hath borne our griefs and carried our sorrows. He was wounded for our transgressions. He was bruised for our iniquities and the chastisement of our peace was upon Him and with His stripes we are healed." This woman, spiritually akin to our Lord, took her daughter's suffering upon herself. But, though she was spiritually akin to Jesus Christ, she was nationally and culturally distant from the God-Man.

The woman was a Canaanite. Jesus was a Jew. And as a Canaanite, she was considered to be a heretic, a heathen and a dog. Jews didn't think much of Canaanites. The Canaanites were considered by the Jews to be sub-human. Biologically, socially, intellectually, and religiously, the Canaanites were considered inferior. They were called dogs, slaves and the scum of the earth. Any Orthodox Jew would turn up his nose at a Canaanite. The Canaanites were despised and rejected. They were excluded and exploited, trampled and disinherited by the Jews.

But not only was this woman a Canaanite, which was more than enough to put her in the class of the despised and the hated, but she lived in Phoenicia, northwest of Palestine, near the coastal cities of Tyre and Sidon. That land is no longer called Phoenicia; we call it Lebanon today. And the bloody hostility between Israel and Lebanon today is but a continuation of the biblical conflict that went on between the Jews and the Phoenicians.

FAITH ALONE

Nationally speaking, this woman's country was at war with the country of Jesus. But this woman came boldly, unashamedly crying to Jesus. A woman different from Him in every respect, except the spiritual kinship by virtue of her vicarious suffering. She had nothing in common with Jesus but faith. She had no other way of approaching Jesus but by faith. Every other fact about her cut her off from him. She had nothing going for her but faith. Every other index in her profile was a barrier, a wall, a partition that separated her from Jesus. But faith alone prevailed; faith alone penetrated the racial myths. Faith alone broke through the cultural barrier. Faith alone leaped over the national wall. Faith alone escaped all the theological and doctrinal objections and got into the heart of Jesus. No wonder Jesus finally said to the woman at the end of this encounter, "O woman, great is thy faith."

Faith alone prevailed, and faith alone will prevail now. We are saved not by doctrine, not by theology, color, culture, class or denomination. We are not saved by works, but we are saved by grace through faith. Faith alone. "Without faith, it is impossible to please God. For he that cometh to God must believe that He is and that He is a rewarder of them that diligently seek him." This woman came to Jesus by faith. She came out of her country and stepped over her nationality by faith alone.

But her faith had another wide river to cross. And that river was the silence of God. In the face of her penetrating cry and her shrieking, shrill, loud, pitiable, awful pleading for help ... God was silent. Jesus answered her not a word.

She did not approach Jesus with soft gentility or dignified demeanor. A long life of hard suffering had eaten away all her pride. She did not wait calmly to get Jesus' attention. She did not raise a courteous finger and wait for Jesus to grant her permission to speak. No, this woman did not hesitate politely. She did not wait for Jesus to turn around and look at her. But she yelled at his back and she clutched at his clothes and she clawed at his garment and yanked at his robe and tugged at his tassel with tears of anguish streaming down her broken face. She cried out loudly, "Have mercy on me O Lord, thou son of David." Her prayer was pitiable, poignant, pathetic, penetrating enough to move the coldest of hearts.

Surely Jesus will turn around and embrace this poor woman and comfort her. Surely Jesus will show His compassion. Surely Jesus will not allow this woman to cry in vain. Didn't Jesus say in His word, "Therefore I say unto you what things ye desire when you pray believe that ye have received them and ye shall have them" (Mark 11:24)? Didn't Jesus say, "Ask and it shall be given, seek and you shall find, knock and it will be opened. For every one who asks receives and he who seeks finds and to him who knocks it will be open" (Luke 11:9,10)? Didn't Jesus say, "If you abide in me and my words abide in you, you shall ask what you will and it shall be done unto you" (John 15:7)? Surely Jesus will keep His word. Surely Jesus will help this woman. Surely God will answer prayer.

HE ANSWERED HER NOT A WORD

But, we are surprised to read that while this woman was yelling at his back and clutching at his clothes and clawing at his cloak, that Jesus answered her not a word, not one word! It's hard to believe, but there it is right there in the first sentence of Matthew 15:23. He didn't say yes, no, wait, maybe. He didn't say anything. He didn't even turn around. He didn't even look at this poor brokenhearted woman. He answered her not a word.

Now that seems mighty out of character with the Christ I know. That seems strange and unusual for the Jesus of love whom we praise. I wonder why the evangelist Matthew left that little sentence in. Why didn't he do like the other evangelist and just leave it out. Why did he leave that little troubling sentence in there to disturb my pat presuppositions about the character and charity of Jesus Christ?

Well, I think there are at least two answers to that question. First, he left it in there because that's what happened. Jesus did not answer her right away. He answered her not a word. That's a rather simple explanation. But that's what happened, and Matthew just told it like it was. Jesus didn't answer the woman.

But, a second reason I think Matthew left this sentence in his account was because he wanted to teach us something about God and about our experience with God. First of all, the silence of God is true to our human experience. In prayer, God is often silent. He answers not a word. Job says in Chapter 19 of his book, "I cry violence, but am not answered. I shout help but there is no redress." God is often silent in the face of human suffering, misery and distress.

SILENT FOR A REASON AND FOR A SEASON

But listen, God remains silent for a season and for a reason. You say, what is the reason for the silence of God? Perhaps it is to give us time to think and to realize that no words from man can save us. Perhaps it is to give our faith room to grow and expand, because faith is sharpened on the stone of unanswered prayer.

Matthew left in the sentence attesting to the silence of Jesus in order to teach us something about the life of prayer. He left it in, in order to teach us something about the mind of God. For silence is often His way of speaking. Doing nothing is often His way of working wonders. Turning His back, He reveals His love. Withdrawing His hand, He heals our hurts.

The disciples didn't understand this. And they got upset with the woman because she kept on hollering and screaming and Jesus kept on walking, not even turning to acknowledge her. And so, as Matthew reports it, they tried to send the woman away. She's crying behind us, and we can't stand it. We've tried to silence her, but she keeps on screaming. We've tried to pull her loose from you, but she keeps on holding to your back. Pull this woman away. Pull yourself away from her, and let's get out of here. The disciples did not understand the silence of Jesus.

They thought that the Master's silence was indifference, and they wanted to cooperate with what they thought was His lack of concern. They thought He was silent because He didn't care. But little did they realize that God can afford to be silent because He has all power in His hands! God is not nervous! God is not weak! He is not insecure! He's not in a hurry! He knows what He can do! He knows what He must do! He knows what He will do!

And so, He doesn't have to talk fast in nervous insecurity. He doesn't have to race against the clock. But He can just take His time, keep His back turned, and keep His mouth shut because He knows His heart is love! His hand is power! His mind is truth! His presence is joy! His spirit is peace! His purpose is to save! He knows who He is, and He knows what He's going to do! So He can just take His time and let sickness run its course. He can let the devil have his say. He can let trouble hang around just a little while. Because,

> God moves in a mysterious way,
> His wonders to perform.
> He plants His footsteps in the sea,

And rides upon the storm.
Deep in unfathomable mines
Of never failing skill,
He treasures up His bright designs
And works His sovereign will.

Ye fearful saints, fresh courage take,
The clouds ye so much dread.
Are big with mercy and shall break
Blessings on your head.
Judge not the Lord by feeble sense,
But trust Him for His grace.
Behind a frowning providence,
He hides a smiling face.

His purpose will ripen fast,
Unfolding every hour.
The bud may have a bitter taste,
But sweet will be the flower.
Blind unbelief is sure to err,
And scan His work in vain.
God is His own interpreter.

Don't worry about the silence of God. He's working all the time. He didn't answer the woman. He answered her not a word. But after a while He looked at her and just said, go home. It's already done; go home. Your daughter is well, and is waiting on you. The problem is solved. The burden is lifted. And her daughter was made whole from that very hour.

He may not answer when you call Him. He may not come when you call Him. But He will answer. He will be there and always on time. Don't throw in the towel! Don't give up hope! Wait on the Lord, and He will strengthen thine heart!

WHERE DO YOU GO
WHEN YOU NEED A MIRACLE?

Text: Matthew 20:1–16   Cheryl Cornish

*W*here do you go when you need a miracle? When the mailbox is full of bills that you can't begin to pay? When the doctor is telling you that your disease can't be healed, that there's no hope? When your children seem determined to self-destruct? Where do you go when you need a miracle?

Most of us turn to the heavens. To the God who listened when we prayed as kids, "Now I lay me down to sleep ...," to the God of our Sunday School years, the God who will take care of us, if we'll only obey Him.

We were taught, there in Sunday School, that the glories of heaven can be ours, someday, if we only use our days on earth well; if we live by the rules; if we take the Commandments to heart; if our spirits are pure. Most of us were taught that if we do right by God, God will do right by us. God in heaven has a reward to give us — has a miracle to share — if we can but muster the faith to get our hands on it.

Perhaps the most preached sermon in the community of Memphis — preached literally over a thousand times — was

Rev. Robert G. Lee's sermon, "Payday Someday."

You can maybe guess the general gist of the sermon. It describes a God who looks a lot like the God you met in Sunday School, a God who has a clear list of rules for you to obey. Obey them, and rewards will come. Disobey them, and punishment will follow. Payday Someday.

It's a message that has been preached a lot because it makes a certain kind of sense to most of us. What's fair is fair. It's a perspective embedded in our religious psyches, whether we want it there or not.

It was there in the minds and hearts of the people of Jesus' day, faithful Jews who were trying their best to follow the rules — who studied the Ten Commandments, who went to Temple, who obeyed the teachers in the synagogue.

These were people who believed in what was fair. They were expectant in their hope of a Messiah. These were people who obeyed the rules here on earth and looked longingly to the heavens for salvation to come, for a miracle to take place here on earth, within their own lives.

And into this whole consciousness, into this world of religious people trying to do all the right things, all the faithful things, all the fair things, comes Jesus. Jesus the Healer. Jesus the Miracle Worker. Jesus the Teacher.

But Jesus seems troubled that so many good folk are waiting for Payday Someday. Waiting for The Day to Come, The Miracle to Happen, they had cast their eyes to heaven. And Jesus wanted them to look right ahead of them, here on earth.

They had geared up for Payday Someday, and lost their sense that God's new creation was among them, here and now; that "the kingdom was among them," that "the glory of God was waiting to be expressed, even in their day."

Jesus is troubled that so many people had sought so hard to find God, and they had looked in all the wrong places, and God had eluded them. And weary from their search, they despaired — having found neither God, nor healing, nor even themselves.

They needed miracles. Their children were sick, and they needed to know why. They, themselves, were crippled, and wondered what it would take for God to heal them. They were lonely and isolated and poor. The Romans were killing them — economically, spiritually, politically, physically.

They needed miracles, and they were looking hard to find them. They were playing by the rules, doing what was right, praying that their persistence would be rewarded. They trusted that somehow, someway, their faithfulness would be rewarded.

So into this whole consciousness came Jesus with the likes of the Parable of the Workers in the Vineyard, and he turned everything on its head. "The last shall be first, and the first shall be last." The workers who have put in only an hour or two in the vineyard will find the same reward as those who have worked all day.

Payday Someday, Jesus says, but maybe the day and the pay are different than you expect. Maybe the day is today, and the pay is more than you'd ever dreamed of in some ways, and less than you ever dreamed of in others. Maybe you have to change your whole perspective before you can appreciate what's come your way. Maybe the pay comes as a totally unexpected miracle — so unexpected that you might miss that it's happened at all.

I have my own, personal image of this story. One of my jobs as a divinity school student was working with autistic teenagers at a wonderful school. Someone had donated a small farm to the school, and the school wanted to start a flower garden. They offered me the job of organizing this garden project over the summer.

I knew that some of the people I'd be working with were very sensitive to colors and smells. I could picture them really enjoying the flower garden project. It really sounded fun to me, too. In fact, I ran with the idea. I talked to a florist in town, and we worked out a deal where the shop would sell and feature flowers grown in our garden.

So, that summer we worked, growing sweet Williams and

zinnias. Rows and rows of them — enough to fill five acres. The colors were beautiful, the stalks were growing long and straight. It was one of the most beautiful summers of my life. The students seemed to love working with the flowers. They were more peaceful and relaxed than I'd ever seen them. And so was I. I felt happy that summer as I boarded the bus to head out to the farm. Everything was going as planned, actually better!

I'd given the flower shop certain dates to expect delivery on our bushels of flowers, and the first date was approaching. We were ready.

I was genuinely excited the day we were to pick our first planting of flowers. I talked with the gardening team, got them all revved up about cutting the flowers, told them how we would be taking them to the flower shop, how beautiful they would look in bouquets, and so forth.

"Today is Flower-Picking Day!" We repeated that directive a hundred times on the bus as we rode out to the farm. And then everybody got off. I got delayed by someone's question, and waved the flower pickers on to the designated field.

I assumed that my students would wait there before they started picking flowers, so that I could give them scissors, show them how long to leave the stems, make sure they could differentiate between the flower and the stalk, and so on and so forth.

But they didn't wait. I had succeeded in getting them so excited about the day's work that they started right in without me. I arrived at the flower garden to a vision that is still in my mind, 13 years after the fact.

The gardeners were running joyfully, wildly, through the garden, grabbing all the blossoms and tossing them in the wind. It was, in its own way, a magnificent sight — deep purple and yellow and red and fuchsia and pink blossoms flying wildly through the air like confetti!

They were almost dancing as they skipped around that garden. "It's Flower-Picking Day!" some of them sang in rhythm.

But I, at first glance, didn't see it as magnificent at all. I saw about $500 worth of flowers in the air, wasted. I saw weeks of work being tossed, literally, to the wind. I saw myself having to explain to the florist shop that the delivery of flowers wouldn't be happening.

I shrieked and screamed at them to stop. But most of them couldn't hear me, and the rest of them didn't want to hear me. All I could do was to stand there and watch. I don't know when I've seen so many flowers floating through the air — hundreds and hundreds of them, it seemed.

I collected myself and my mood as I stared. They all looked so happy. The sky was so blue. And this was not in the least how I'd anticipated things would turn out.

But gradually, a truth dawned within me, and to this day I cherish the image of those kids and the flowers and the day itself. Of the spontaneous celebration of what had been a wonderful time together — a genuine labor of love and friendship.

The point of the flower garden, after all, was not so much the flowers, but our being there in the garden together, and loving the feel of the earth and the beautiful colors around us, and the smell of the air, and the chance to create something wonderful.

Which is exactly what we had done. That vision of those kids dancing through the garden, joyfully throwing the blossoms, happy to be there and with each other, really was a sight to behold.

The gardeners were in touch with some important truths about the world. They knew, more intuitively than I, that the point of the garden was being there, in the midst of it, loving it, tending it that the garden didn't point to a reality beyond itself — but was the reality. That if there was reward to be had, it was a reward to be claimed there, in the earth, with the flowers themselves — not from the florist shop, not from the pay, not from the met expectation.

"The kingdom of God is among us!" they seemed to proclaim as they joyfully tossed those flowers. The new creation in our midst.

Which is, I think, Jesus' point in this parable. Something is terribly amiss, spiritually, if we find ourselves resentfully trying to do the right thing, supposedly for the sake of God, if we're trying to tough it out until the end in order to receive some reward.

So many of us, even with our good intentions, search in the wrong direction for the wrong God, and we end up finding neither God nor ourselves.

Payday Someday, we tell ourselves. Hard work will have its rewards. Seeing God as a taskmaster to be pleased, we keep our nose to the grindstone, thinking of that day when the reward will come.

Seeing God as a rewarder of the just and a punisher of the wicked, we wonder what's gone wrong when we've followed the rules and the payoff isn't what we expected.

When we've worked 12 hours in the hot sun for what we've achieved, and those who have barely struggled seem to flourish. Like the workers in the parable, we feel a kind of rage at a God whose love doesn't know the same boundaries that ours does:

A God who rewards those who, in our minds, don't deserve it.
A God who doesn't intervene to change things that we desperately want changed.
A God who doesn't give rewards and punishments according to what we've done.

What does God owe us, after all? Shouldn't there be rules, somehow? A system to follow?

I don't know. I do know this. I know that life isn't fair, according to traditional ways of reasoning it. I know that good people often suffer, greatly and unfairly. I know that wonderful parents sometimes lose their children. I know that virtuous, kindly people often find their lives turned upside down by the onset of a disease. I know that tornadoes destroy the houses of the faithful as well as the houses of the wicked.

Life isn't fair according to the traditional rules. You know it. I know it.

But life is very, very good. And life is sacred, and life is where God is. Among us now. In our midst.

Margaret Fuller, the great philosopher, is quoted as saying, "I accept the universe." Thomas Carlyle, her contemporary, responded to that statement by saying, "Well, by God, she'd better!"

And finally, we'd all better. This insistence on what "should be," what God ought to do, what life ought to bring us, finally has to fade in light of what life is.

But the challenge in that is, then, to really discern what life is, and that, of course, is where faith comes in.

You know, when my niece, Madaleine Claire, was born with Down's syndrome, our family was really thrown into a tailspin. Down's syndrome was supposed to be one of those diseases that happened to other people's kids. It shouldn't happen. Not to anybody. Not to us.

But it did. And one of the fascinating things was to see how everyone struggled to come up with an explanation, a way to name how this situation had been earned.

People would politely inquire as to my sister Eileen's age or her drinking habits. "Why had she not had an amniocentesis?" they would ask. Questions that implied blame — questions that looked for how this could have been prevented and made them think it could never happen to them because they played by the rules.

And in the other camp were those who implied that this birth was a particular sign of God's blessing. "God sends special kids to special families," people would say.

That was infinitely preferable to the other camp in terms of expressing support, but as Mitch and Eileen joked, it's a little scary to imply that if you're good at parenting, God will reward your efforts by sending plagues upon your children. Many people would not consider that much of an incentive program.

It's interesting to see how, in the face of a surprise in life, when our system of behaviors and rewards breaks down, we still hunt, desperately, for an explanation, a statement of blame or praise, rather than simply letting life be as it is and allowing God's grace to work.

There's a wonderful story about an old woman who lived out in the woods. Stories ran wild about her. She was considered by some people to be a witch, even. Children in the small village nearby were puzzled by her — especially the stories of her great wisdom. So one day, they decided to try to fool her.

They found a baby bird. One of the little boys cupped it in his hands and said to his friends, "We'll ask her whether the bird I have in my hands is dead or alive. If she says it's dead, I'll open my hands and let it fly away. If she says it's alive, I'll crush it in my hands, and she'll see that it's dead."

And the children went to the old woman and presented her with this puzzle. "Old woman," the little boy asked, "this bird in my hands — is it dead or alive?"

The old woman became very still, studied the boy's hands, and then looked at him carefully.

"It's in your hands," she said.

And so it is. As much as we might wish that weren't the case. Is a child with Down's syndrome a blessing to our society or a curse? That decision is in our hands.

It will depend on how we treat her, what we see in her, how clear and how loving our vision can be as we look at her.

It's in our hands. How to deal with racial and ethnic diversity, differences in background, differences in experience — blessings or curses? It's in our hands.

How to deal with surprises in life — unexpected turns, unanticipated outcomes. Blessings or curses? It's in our hands.

How to define life and faith itself? We can limit our faith so that it's a faith of Payday Someday — of making, arbitrarily, a contract with God and trying to earn some reward. Or we can accept that Christ is present with us, and celebrate this as a day alive with the grace of God — a day when we toss flowers and celebrate joyfully the generosity of a God whose love goes beyond what we ever expected to see.

It's in our hands — to turn this day into a day of blessing, a day where God's grace is freely present between and among us — or a day of curse, where we name "haves" and "have nots," where we decide who has earned their keep and who hasn't.

Where do you go when you need a miracle? Where do you go when things are so bad that there's no way to keep going?

You go to the problem itself, with the faith that even though the situation may not be changed magically, immediately, you still have the opportunity to find healing there. We may not be able to heal our illness, but we are always able to find healing for our lives.

Where do you go when you need a miracle? You go to the depths of your heart and soul, where that inner voice of God exists, that inner voice of love, and you cling to it. You give up the old expectations about what your life should be, and you take a step in faith, even when you can't see what's in front of you. You trust that God can expand your heart, your eyes, your understandings, your faith, to embrace what you have to.

Religious leaders in ancient societies — shamans or medicine people — believed that an illness or an injury, whether of the body or of the spirit, was an opportunity to make your life better than before.

Dis-ease, dis-order, offered the chance to rethink life, to reassess priorities, to name what we most hungered for or needed. An illness can be a time when we are challenged in new ways, with new intensity, to make our outer lives harmonize with our inner values.

Illness forces us to listen to our lives, to name our stresses, our fears, our sources of support, our joys. It draws attention to who we are, at our most basic, physical point of being.

I recently talked with a man who lives with AIDS. He said that the question for him had become not "How do I die?" but rather, "What makes me live?" He said that AIDS had taught him that he could choose to make each day sacred, that he could listen each day to God's voice of love within him and ignore, if need be, messages that had no redemption, no compassion, no love in them.

Jesus was a healer, a worker of miracles. But the miracles came in ways that no one expected. They came in the midst of a troubled city, in the midst of troubled lives, in desperate moments that suddenly taught an unexpected truth.

They came, not as the reward of years of hard and faithful living, but often by surprise and often in the midst of suffering. They came when people had the courage to put away the old rule books — and to let life take a new, totally unexpected direction.

Whenever our life becomes precarious — through difficult situations, through disease — we have the opportunity to throw away our old rule books. We can embrace the opportunity to live more richly, to become who we are in a more authentic way by listening to the voice of God within us.

Love is the greatest healing force known in the world. I have heard love described as being "the fuel of our souls." It will keep people alive when physicians predict that death is imminent. It will bring out truths and life-giving insights from within us that give us the strength to continue for another day.

In learning to trust that our lives are miraculous, learning to generate love for ourselves, to receive the love that is ours through God, to accept and ask for the love of others, we grow in our awareness of the miracle that is life, of the miracle that carries us even through physical death into new life.

There's an old joke about a man who had a yard full of dandelions. He was desperate to get rid of them so that his lawn could be full of beautiful, green grass. He tried herbicide after herbicide. He devoted hours to pulling the weeds by hand.

Finally, in frustration, he wrote the USDA — the U.S. Department of Agriculture — and said, "Do you have anything to suggest for me to try to control these dandelions?"

The letter came back on official stationery: "Dear Mr. Jones, We suggest that you learn to love them."

Where do you look for a miracle? You stare at the weeds of your life, and you listen to your heart. You trust that God can help you see the dandelions with new eyes and see what there is in that situation to love.

We may find that the miracle in our lives is not in the removal of an unexpected intruder — whether it be a virus, a cancer, a depression. The miracle may come in our learning to love the dandelions in our life because they helped our vision expand so that we could learn to love our lives in a new way. We may come to trust with new depth the holiness of God, the joy of being human and our communion with God. **AMEN**.

THE INTERRUPTIONS

Text: Mark 5:21–43   James S. Lowry

"Talitha cumi ,"
    he said to the little girl.
        She wasn't but twelve years old.
        In those days little girls lived on the margins.
        Nobody cared much for children back then …
            especially they didn't care for little girls.
        Except …
            except for this little girl's daddy.
        Her daddy loved her a lot.
        So did Jesus.
        For her daddy and for Jesus
            this little girl was not at the margin …
                oh no …
        she was special.
    She was at the center.
    Jesus took the little girl by the hand.

"Talitha cumi,"
    he said in Aramaic.
        That's the language she spoke.
        It means little girl, get up.
        She was dead.
        She got up all the same.

That's the way of it, for us.
For the church, it's a picture of the way things are.
If we can just keep our minds from being too
　　technical, it's a picture of resurrection
　　drawn by Jesus and saved by Mark.

Wonder if Pappy heard anything like that.
Of course it wouldn't have been "talitha cumi."
Pappy wasn't a little girl,
　　but, then,
　　　I haven't the slightest idea
　　　what the Aramaic might be for <u>old man, get up</u>,
　　　but I'm sure Pappy heard it
　　　and I'm sure Pappy got up.

For Pappy there wasn't much warning.
It was a Sunday morning …
Palm Sunday to be exact.
Ate breakfast.
Got ready for church.
Almost forgot the special offering
　　they were taking that Sunday;
　　but at the last minute remembered,
　　wrote a check and put it in his pocket.

　　　　The special offering was for a project
　　　　　to help poor people become self-sufficient.

On the way to church
　　Pappy had a heart attack and died.
Car just drifted off the road,
　　down a bank
　　and came to rest in a thicket of honeysuckle.
Mama wasn't hurt at all
　　except for a broken heart …

lifelong sweethearts those two.

Wonder if Pappy heard the Savior say
    something like

    <u>talitha cumi</u>.

I'm sure of it,
    except the Savior surely said it in English.
Pappy didn't speak a word of Aramaic,
    and it surely must have been
        old man, get up,
        and I'm sure Pappy got up ...
        absolutely sure of it ...
        there in the honeysuckle thicket
        on the side of the road.

But that's the way the story ends, isn't it?
In the church
    that's always the way the story ends.
It's one of the advantages of telling stories in church.
We tell all of our stories
    knowing from the beginning
    how the stories will end.

    The mystery in the church
        is not how our stories end.
    All of our stories end
        with the Savior saying <u>get up</u>.
    The mystery in the church
        is how our stories begin,
        and how our stories play out to the end.
Take the story of Jairus' daughter as an example.
It's a story of an interruption
    which itself begins with an interruption:

A kind of interruption within an interruption,
    as it were.
What ever shall we do with these desperate people
who are forever interrupting the church
as we go about the important matters of our truth dealing.

The truth in which we deal
    is of great and lasting consequence.
What, then,
    shall we do with these people
    who interrupt our dealing with truth?

Can you imagine it?
Can you imagine,
    there I was
    just as I was beginning to work on this sermon ...
    this sermon on interruptions
    when what should happen,
    but like a piece of living poetry,
    they buzzed up to my office on the
    intercom saying there was a man on the phone
    who wanted a handout.
    He had tried to reach me all day the day before
        when I was away ...
        a real pest this one.

I tried to hide my annoyance at the
    interruption but was aware, of course,
    of the poetic irony that was playing out ...
    my sermon on interruptions was being interrupted.

        "This is Jim Lowry.
        How can I help?"
        "Are you the Senior Pastor?"

HOPE AND HEALING

"Yes, I am."

"My name is (and he told me his name
    but I don't remember it).
Do you remember me?
I worshipped at Idlewild about two years ago."

"No, I'm sorry. I don't remember."

"Well, I'm passing through town again.
I'm HIV positive and need help getting to Canada
    where they have socialized medicine."

I've been at this preaching business a long time,
    and it sounded like a con to me,
    but on the outside chance he was telling me the truth,
    I began to explain ways and procedures
    by which we are able to help people.
Whether he read my words as a rejection
    or an exposé — we'll never know.
        He called me a name that shouldn't be repeated
        and slammed down the phone.

I went back to writing my sermon on interruptions,
    haunted.
I'm almost certain he was a con ...
    almost.
If, however,
    by some chance,
    he was telling the truth
    and I did not welcome him,
    by what hypocrisy
        was I to write this sermon ...
        by what hypocrisy
        or by what forgiving grace?

At least I knew this text on interruptions
deals with no minor matter.

Anyway,
back to the story of Jairus' daughter ...
a story to which we know the ending.
Strange, isn't it,
that Mark saved the name of Jairus for us,
but didn't save the name of his daughter?
Like I said,
little girls lived on the margins in those days,
but that was then
and this is now.

My daughters' names are
Jayne Stallworth Lowry and
Anne Nichols Lowry,
and I have their names written down
right here ...
daddies don't ever forget.

The story begins with the pleading of a despairing daddy
interrupting Jesus ...
as Jesus was living and teaching important matters of
truth.
The crowd was pressing in ...
hungry for important matters of truth:

This is the way God is ...
This is what God does ...
This is what God thinks. ...
Those were the matters of consequence
with which Jesus and the church were dealing
as they and we shuttled back and forth from place to place,
but then

they were interrupted ...
interrupted by a desperate daddy.

"Come quick; my little girl is dying."

Wonder if Jesus thought he just might be a con?
Don't forget though.
We know how the story is going to end.
We always know how our stories end.
Jesus dropped everything and went.
That's how the story plays out.
It's always how the story plays out for Jesus.
I wish the man hadn't hung up.
I wish I could remember his name.
I wish I had not sounded so ...
    so bureaucratic.

Anyway,
    away they went
    with the crowd in tow ...
    pushing and shoving ...
    groping after matters of truth;
    but Jesus put the whole truth of the church on hold
    and went chasing to the bedside of this little no-name girl ...

        except her daddy knew her name
        and so did Jesus, I bet.
            Shame on Mark for not remembering her name.
Then,
    wouldn't you know it?
On the way to the little girl's bedside,
    before the story could play to its end,
    they were interrupted again ...

    an interruption of the interruption, as it were.

This time it was a no-name woman.

Whatever shall we do with this desperate no-name woman
    who interrupts the church
    while the church is in pursuit of its interruptions?

        Unclean is what she was.
        A twelve-year hemorrhage.
        Not only did she feel unclean,
            by religion and custom,
            she was declared to be unclean.
        Whatever she touched,
            by religious law,
            was contaminated and,
            by ritual,
            had to be cleansed;
                and there she was,
                groping through the crowd
                to touch the hem of Jesus' garment.

I hope the most desperate among us
    don't grow so cynical
    that they stop groping through the crowd
    to interrupt the church
    as we play out our story to its end.

I also hope the church doesn't grow so cynical
    that it refuses to be interrupted by the
    desperate among us as we play our story to its end.
        "Who touched me?" asked Jesus.
        "What do you mean?" said the disciples.
        "Can't you see the crowd?"

        "I didn't ask who shoved me;
            I asked who touched me."

I made up some of that part;
    but it is hard for the church,
    sometimes,
      to tell the difference in a shove and a touch.

"I did," said the desperate no-name woman.
"Daughter, your faith has made you well ...
    go in peace."

    She may have had no name worth remembering
      but Jesus called her <u>daughter</u>.

Meanwhile,
    the little girl died;
    and isn't that the way of it(?);
    but we know how the story ends.

    <u>Talitha cumi.</u>

    "Little girl, get up."

      It's the way the story ends.
      It's a picture drawn by Jesus
        and saved by Mark ...
        a picture of how the story ends ...
      of how the church's story always ends.

This is what I think it means:
If you are desperate
    and,
    for whatever reason,
    you are hanging on the margins,
      then,
      by all means,
      interrupt the church
      in all of our truth dealing.

We are here playing our story to its end
    trying desperately by word and deed
      as best we can to speak and live the truth of God
        by living and teaching
        what God is like and
        what God is doing and
        what God is thinking.

If you are desperate,
    for whatever reason,
    interrupt the Church of Jesus Christ.
      It is through your interruption
      that you have a chance for healing,
      and it is through your interruptions
      that the truth given the church
      will ever make much sense
      or make any real difference.

But there's more:
If you are the Church of Jesus Christ
    (and you are the Church of Jesus Christ ...
    if you are the Church of Jesus Christ)
      trying desperately as best you can
      to speak and live the truth of God
      as you play our story to its end
      then be prepared ...
      get ready
      to be interrupted ...
      to be stopped in your tracks
      by all manner of desperate people.
        It is through our interruptions
          that the truth given us will ever matter much.

In fact,
      it is largely through interruptions
      that our story plays to its end.

Knowing how the story ends
   gives us freedom to play the story well.

We know how the story ends, don't we?

     <u>Talitha Cumi</u>.

SICKNESS AND SIN: HOW DID JESUS RESPOND? HOW DOES HE CALL US TO RESPOND?

Text: Matthew 4:23–24   John Sartelle

---

*J*esus went throughout Galilee, teaching in their synagogues, preaching the good news of the kingdom, and healing every disease and sickness among the people. News about him spread all over Syria, and people brought to him all who were ill with various diseases, those suffering severe pain, the demon possessed, those having seizures, and the paralyzed, and he healed them.   (Matthew 4:23–24)

Here came Jesus. He suddenly broke on the scene. Unexpected. No one knew He was coming. Just another preacher? No. He preached like no one they had ever heard. Not even John the Baptist could preach like Jesus did. But He was doing something no one had ever done. He was healing. And He was doing it on a massive scale. He was healing every disease He encountered. When He saw a blind man, He made him see. When He saw a paralyzed man, He made him walk. He didn't pray for the person's healing. He just spoke a word, and the person was healed. It was as if the disease had to obey Him.

We let passages like Matthew 4:23–24 slip by us unnoticed. It describes His early ministry in general and does not mention specific persons or tell a particular story. So we usually skip over such passages and treat them as transitions. But these verses describe events that were dynamic and powerful.

Look at verse 25. News about Him spread quickly, even to the foreign countries. And here they came. The crowds would not let Him rest. They came to listen, to be healed, and to watch. They came from Syria, from the Decapolis, from Jerusalem, Judea, and the Transjordan.

For the next few minutes I want us to watch Jesus the Healer as He encountered a sick and sinful world. I want us to watch what He did, why He did it, and to ask what Jesus calls us to do as we face sickness in the world around us.

And there is sickness all around us. David Hume wrote 200 years ago: "Were a stranger to drop suddenly into this world I would show him a specimen of its ills — a hospital full of diseases, a prison crowded with criminals, a nation languishing under tyranny, famine, or pestilence." Even though David Hume was a skeptic, he was recognizing in those words a biblical truth: We live in a fallen world, a world with a natural inclination to sin and besieged by sickness and death.

We want to insulate ourselves from the pain, hurt, and sickness in the world around us. We want to hide from it. We want to turn our heads and walk around it. But look at Jesus in this passage. He faced it head on. He did not turn away or try to avoid it. He didn't put on rose-colored glasses and pretend it wasn't there. And He won't let us do that either. But we are getting ahead of ourselves.

Let's watch as He healed these people and first see the **motivation** of the Healer. There are three words that will tell us what motivated Jesus to heal the sickness He saw.

JOHN SARTELLE

VERIFICATION

He healed the sickness around Him to verify His claims to be the Son of God. We read in Matthew 9:2–7:

> Some men brought to him a paralytic, lying on a mat. When Jesus saw their faith, he said to the paralytic, "Take heart, son; your sins are forgiven." At this, some of the teachers of the law said to themselves, "This fellow is blaspheming!" Knowing their thoughts, Jesus said, "Why do you entertain evil thoughts in your hearts? Which is easier: to say, 'Your sins are forgiven,' or to say, 'Get up and walk?' But so that you may know that the Son of Man has authority on earth to forgive sins ... " Then he said to the paralytic. "Get up, take your mat and go home." And the man got up and went home.

Jesus was saying it Himself: "I am healing this paralyzed man so that you will know that I am who I say I am. I am the Son of God, and I have the power to forgive sins." The healing was a verification of His deity.

Verification is also our motivation as Jesus calls us to participate in His healing ministry. The healing ministry of the church verifies that we belong to Him. Jesus has told us. He has told the world. Unless we are involved in healing this sick and sinful world, we have nothing to do with Him. Read Matthew 25:34–36:

> Then the King will say to those on his right, "Come, you who are blessed by my Father; take your inheritance, the kingdom prepared for you since the creation of the world. For I was hungry and you gave me something to eat, I was thirsty and you gave me something to drink, I was a stranger and you invited me in,

I needed clothes and you clothed me, I was sick and you looked after me, I was in prison and you came to visit me."

Jesus was saying that our healing ministry to a sick and hurting world verifies that we are with Him. Jesus was a healer in the broadest sense of the term. He has called us to follow Him — to be healers in every way we can in a world of pain and disease.

Who are the healers? Doctors, nurses, ministers, elders, deacons, all Christians who pray for the sick, help those who are hurting, care for the wounded, encourage the depressed, hold the dying, and weep in sympathy for those in pain — all who do so in the name of Christ are healers. And if we are not doing these things in some way, we have no right to claim to be with Him.

The first word that describes Jesus' motivation as a healer is **verification**.

CONSOLATION

Consolation is a compassion that brings comfort. When Jesus saw the sickness and pain, He was motivated to heal by His compassion in order to bring comfort. Read Matthew 20:30–34:

Two blind men were sitting by the roadside, and when they heard that Jesus was going by, they shouted, "Lord, Son of David, have mercy on us!" The crowd rebuked them and told them to be quiet, but they shouted all the louder, "Lord, Son of David, have mercy on us!" Jesus stopped and called them. "What do you want me to do for you?" he asked. "Lord," they answered, "we want our sight." Jesus had compassion on them and touched their eyes. Immediately they received their sight and followed him.

Jesus was motivated to heal by His compassion. Jesus was not an automaton, a robot God saying, "I've got to do this to prove to these people who I am." Jesus felt for these folks. I would love to have seen Jesus' face at that moment. I would have seen a picture of compassion.

I want to tell you something. This is just an aside. When we pray for some sort of healing from our hurting, sometimes He chooses not to heal. But His compassion is always there. Look at His face in your pain, and you will always see compassion.

For years my father had Alzheimer's Disease. He was in a hospital in Montgomery, Alabama, for over a year. A brilliant scholar, he did not even know I was his son. A football player and Marine, he lost both legs to blood poisoning while in the hospital. Did we pray for God to heal him? Yes. Did He? No. He did not heal him from Alzheimer's. He did not save his legs. But every step of the way Jesus gave us consolation. Every step of the way, we saw His compassion as He answered prayers, provided medical care from unexpected sources, and drew the family closer together.

This is the same consolation that Jesus demands we give to those around us when He calls us to follow Him. What does He say that we are to do with the comfort we receive from Him?

> Praise be to the God and Father of our Lord Jesus Christ, the Father of compassion and the God of all comfort, who comforts us in all our troubles, so that we can comfort those in any trouble with the comfort we ourselves have received from God. (2 Corinthians 1:3–4)

What are we to do with the consolation Jesus gives us in our sickness? We are to use that same consolation in the healing of others.

Brennan Manning tells the story of Dominique, who was living the life of a Christian ascetic with Christian brothers in

St. Remy, France. He was 6'2", muscular and strong. But at the age of 54 he was dying of inoperable cancer. With the permission of the brothers in his community, he moved to a poor neighborhood of Paris and took a job as a night watchman in a factory. After working all night, each morning he would go to a park across from his apartment. He would spend the day there. Hanging around in a poor area with the marginal people, drifters, winos, "has beens," and cynical, dirty, old men, Dominique never criticized, scolded, or reprimanded them for their attitude, language, and filthy stories. He told them good stories, shared his food, and accepted them where they were. He said nothing of Christ until they wanted to know what made him so different. Their bitterness and cynicism began to disappear. Their language changed. Their sordid stories stopped. He stayed there with those folks, healing them, until he died. When they found his body in the apartment, this note was found in his diary:

> All that is not the love of God has no meaning to me. I can truthfully say that I have no interest in anything but the love of God which is in Christ Jesus. If God wants it to, my life will be useful through my word, and virtues. If He wants it to, my life will bear fruit through my prayers and sacrifices. But the usefulness of my life is His concern, not mine. It would be indecent of me to worry about that.

What was he saying? "I am going to love and care like Christ. I will leave how He uses it to Him." Dominique was using the consolation he had received from Jesus all of his life to heal that poor and hurting community in Paris.

The first two words that describe what motivated Jesus to heal are **verification** and **consolation**.

LIBERATION

Jesus was liberating the world around Him from the effects of sin, Satan, and sickness.

Go back to our text, and read Matthew 4:23, "Jesus went throughout Galilee, teaching in their synagogues, preaching the good news of the kingdom, and healing **every** disease and sickness among the people."

The emphasis is on "every." This was not something Jesus did occasionally. Wherever He saw despair, sickness and the results of the fall, He gave Satan and sin no quarter. Because of the fall, people were blind. Because of the fall, people were paralyzed. Because of the fall, people were deaf. Because of the fall, people died. When Jesus met blind people, He made them see. When He met paralyzed people, He made them walk. When Jesus met deaf people, He made them hear. When Jesus met a funeral procession, He raised the dead. He liberated people from the result of Man's sin.

One of my favorite hymns is "Joy to the World." The third verse speaks of the liberating power of the gospel: "No more let sins and sorrows grow, nor thorns infest the ground; He comes to make His blessings flow far as the curse is found." Darkness disappears when light breaks in. Wherever He went, wherever He saw sin's awful work — He began to reverse the effects of the fall. That is what we are doing. He has called His people to be salt and light in this fallen, sinful, and sick world. Everywhere we go we should be reversing the effects of the fall in the name of Christ.

What motivated Jesus to heal the world around Him? **Verification, consolation,** and **liberation.**

But I don't want to leave this subject until we look at the text one more time and understand that the better healing is not the healing of the body — the better healing is the healing of the soul. Read Matthew 4:23, "Jesus went throughout Galilee, teaching in their synagogues. preaching the good news of the kingdom, and healing every disease and sickness among the people."

The good news of the kingdom was not that people could be healed physically. The good news of the kingdom was that people could be healed spiritually. There were many people in that crowd who were healed physically and yet missed the greater healing.

This is powerful. For many years I had talked to a man about his sin and his need of a Saviour. He could not see or understand what sin was doing to his life. One day he came to me and asked me to pray for him. He had come straight from his doctor's office and had just received the news that he had cancer. What an irony! For years he had been told that he had cancer of the soul and had paid no attention. But he literally ran to me, wanting me to pray that God would heal him of cancer in his body. He was still missing the healing that he needed the most — the healing of his heart from sin.

Think about every person that Jesus physically healed in that period described in the verses we read. Folks, every one of them finally died. After Jesus healed them, they may have lived 60 more years. But every one of them eventually died.

It is the good news of the kingdom that tells us that even though we die, yet shall we live (John 11:25). The good news of the kingdom tells us that Jesus died for our sins. The good news of the kingdom tells us that "to be absent from the body is to be present with the Lord" (2 Corinthians 5:8). The good news of the kingdom tells us that the Holy Spirit has changed our hearts and restored the relationship with our Maker. He has healed our souls. That healing is the better healing.

My friend John Reisinger is a wonderful Baptist minister. When he was in the South Pacific in the service, no one would have ever guessed he would become a Christian, much less a minister. In a church he served, there was a special child with Down's syndrome. His name was David. David would sit on the front pew and listen to every sermon. John Reisinger was his preacher. He would not listen to any of the ministers on television because Pastor John was HIS preacher. Every Sunday David would give his minister a hug. One evening after church John picked up the little boy and said, "David, you don't realize what I am saying to you right now, but one day Jesus is going to set you beside all the Huxleys and Bertrand Russells of this world and prove to all of history that you understood more than they did."

Many people would have looked at David and thought his mind needed healing. But in reality David knew more than the brilliant Huxley and Russell. There are blind people who see more than folks with 20/20 vision. Their spiritual blindness has been healed. And there are other people who can see, who are spiritually blind to Jesus and His work in the world all around them. The better healing is the healing of the soul. The better healing is the healing that takes away our spiritual blindness, our spiritual deafness and our spiritual paralysis.

DON'T LET 'EM CHEAT IT OUT OF YOU!

J. Peter Sartain

One afternoon not long ago I received word that an elderly friend, dying of cancer in a local nursing home, was asking to see me. That evening I enjoyed a spirited half-hour visit in her darkened room. She's 88 years old and just a wisp of her former self, but she's full of life and wisdom and love for God. Because she's hard-of-hearing we had a rather loud conversation, all of it within earshot of her roommate — who insisted that we were not bothering her, and who kept suggesting that we turn on a light to be able to see better. Knowing that the only light available was a harsh fluorescent ceiling panel, my friend and I gratefully declined. At the end of my visit I stopped by the roommate's bed to say "good night" to her as well.

I was expecting to offer a brief farewell, to tell her that I would pray for her, too. But she stopped me in my tracks by offering some stunning advice.

Taking my arm and gently stroking it several times, she looked squarely at me with tired but penetrating eyes and said very softly, "You're so young and happy and good. Always stay that way. Don't ever let 'em cheat it out of you."

I knew exactly what she meant. She wasn't referring to any

person, but to the hardships of life and the suffering that accompanies them. In other words, "Don't let any hard times cheat you out of happiness by making you bitter; don't let anger get hold of you and make you dwell on the negative; don't let illness sap you of your hope or faith. Don't let anything like that cheat you out of happiness and goodness." Her words have found a permanent place on my heart since that brief encounter.

Jesus knew well the difficulties of life. He met with rejection and misunderstanding. People were out to get him! On the cross he was sad, discouraged and abandoned; his body was racked with agonizing pain. Yet he did not give in to bitterness over his predicament; he continued to pursue love and forgiveness, and as St. Paul wrote, "He gave himself for us as an offering to God, a gift of pleasing fragrance" (Ephesians 5:2). Jesus did not let the terrible assaults on his life cheat him out of his love for the Father, nor did he let the difficulties he faced cheat him out of his love for us. Instead, out of the midst of his suffering he gave us hope.

It seems to me that one of the virtues most sorely needed today is hope. Sometimes life just seems overwhelming; we look at the world situation and ask ourselves, "Where do you even begin to sort it out, to put things on the right track?" We look at the economy, the rising cost of health care, and we ask a similar question: "How in the world will we ever tackle the challenge of health care in a way that will honestly help people for the long haul?" Or perhaps we look at our own lives when afflicted with illness and ask ourselves, "How will I ever pay my medical bills? Will I ever be well again? And if I'm not to be well again, will I be a burden on my family? How will God heal me?"

Being overwhelmed by such thoughts can paralyze us; we don't know where to begin, how to get from here to there so we do nothing. We wish we had a different attitude, that we were "hopeful," but the attitude doesn't seem to come. We might even begin to feel guilty because we're worried, and then we pray, "I'm sorry, God, that I don't have more faith. I must not be a very good Christian because my faith is so weak that I worry too much." And then there's the anger, welling up from frustration and worry. "What did I do to deserve this? Why does God treat me this way?" A vicious cycle — but a very natural one.

Perhaps we mistakenly think of hope simply as a positive attitude, something akin to natural optimism, or as a "feeling" we have to conjure up on our own steam. And then perhaps in our darker moments, we fear our lack of hope is sinful — a thought that only mires us more deeply in confusion, one that makes the cycle seem even more vicious.

But hope does not begin with us. Hope begins with God: His unfailing love and care for us, expressed most fully in Jesus, and his absolute understanding of the trials we face, demonstrated by Jesus' willingness to die on the cross. It was because of his total confidence in the loving care of his Father that Jesus was able to tell his disciples, "Do not live in fear, little flock. It has pleased your Father to give you the kingdom" (Luke 12:32). True hope is based not on a feeling but on the truth. And the deepest truth of life is this: God so loves the world that he gave his only son, his most precious possession, to us (John 3:16), and absolutely nothing, "neither trial, nor distress" (Romans 8), can separate us from his love and care. No one believed that truth more firmly than Jesus.

What's more, the suffering we undergo makes God turn toward us all the more: for seeing the pain in our faces he sees the face of Jesus, his only son.

Remember the story of "doubting Thomas" (John 20), who was not present the first time the risen Jesus appeared in the upper room? What did he want as proof that Jesus was real? He wanted to touch Jesus' wounds, to see the fragile body marked by the soldiers' blows and the detractors' insults, the holes of the nails and the incision of the lance! He wanted to see Jesus' wounds! And seeing the wounds, he believed. Seeing the wounds, he hoped.

One of the marvelous ironies of Christian faith is the knowledge that just when our suffering causes us to feel alienated from Jesus, hope helps us realize that in fact our suffering makes us more like Jesus! And what did the Father do, as he saw his son willingly undergo the cross and give himself to suffering and death for our sake? He raised him up, he glorified him, he gave him renewed and resurrected life! Jesus was the man of hope, because he trusted that no matter what life gave him, his heavenly Father would bring even greater life out of it. He knew that's the way his Father is! He was not disappointed, and neither will we be. In our suffering we draw close to Jesus, and turning his face toward us, our heavenly Father sees the face of his son, whom he loves. He longs to heal our wounds, to take us beyond the kind of life we knew before to an even fuller life. What exactly is the kind of healing God wants for us? That's for him to teach us, but we can stake our lives on this: God knows our needs, he has felt our suffering in his son, and in his best and most loving way he will share his life with us — he will heal us.

> There was once a sculptor working hard with his hammer and chisel on a large block of marble. A little boy who was watching him saw nothing more than large and small pieces of stone falling away left and right. He had no idea what was happening. But when the boy returned to the studio a few weeks later, he saw to his great surprise a large, powerful lion sitting in the place where the marble had stood. With great excitement the boy ran to the sculptor and said, "Sir, how did you know there was a lion in the marble?"

I marvel at the creative genius of artists! They have the enviable gift of a deeper vision of life, the ability to see through surface appearances to profound beauty. In one mass of marble, Michelangelo saw a loving mother caressing her dead son's lifeless body; in another, a self-assured David about to hurl a stone at the powerful Goliath; and in another, an angry Moses about to rise from his seat in protest against a faithless people. Michelangelo saw form and life where there was none. The sculptor in my little story saw a lion where others could see only a block of stone.

Great artists are blessed with creative vision. But as penetrating as their vision may be, it remains only a shadow of the loving and creative glance God turns our way at all times. God sees with his heart, and as he looks our way he sees not a mass of anonymous faces, but children he loves uniquely and deeply, lives he wants to share. And his glance is turned to us especially when we suffer.

Perhaps when illness wracks our body all we see are the effects of the illness — the scars and disfigurements, the disquieting pain or the (feared?) poor prognosis. But what does God see?

God sees life — vital and precious life, his own image and likeness, the human face of his son. And fixing his gaze ever so gently on our aching bodies and weary hearts, he loves us with a healing love more pure than any we've ever known. The same loving God who gave us life will not let illness or suffering cheat us out of the life he has given us, and the life he has in store for us! And if that seems to be the case, it's only because he has even greater life to create for us and within us!

God never turns his back on his own image and likeness, the very face of his son. He longs only to give us life — life to the full. That's a word of truth worth hoping our lives on. Nothing can cheat us out of God's longing to give us life!

SAID I WASN'T GONNA TELL NOBODY!

Text: Mark 1:35–45   Kenneth S. Robinson

And there came a leper to him, beseeching him, and kneeling down to him, and saying unto him, "If thou wilt, thou canst make me clean."   (Mark 1:40)

Jesus' healings had become legendary; His fame was spreading contagiously. One morning, following prayer, Simon and the disciples informed Him that figuratively "everybody" was looking for Him; "all men seek for thee." But as Jesus moved on to the next town — to the next mass of hopefuls — there was surely one man who must have been looking for the Lord even more diligently than most; for we read, "There came a leper **beseeching**" Him. More than anybody else, this leper knew that Jesus was his only hope. He'd already been to the priests; they'd seen the depressed plaques, the white skin and hair, the scabs, and had invoked the presumption of leprosy. He'd already complied with the diagnostic test of quarantine. He'd already tried the prescribed ritual cleansings. Yet all the signs of the disease — the blanching, the baldness, the raw sores — remained, and the priests were required to declare him "unclean." As mandated by the Levitical Codes, the brother's face was covered, and he was relegated to dwelling alone — outside of the camp. So, while he pressed his way toward the One who embodied his only hope, I can almost hear the leper singing, "When you've tried everything and everything has failed, try Jesus!"

Knowing his situation and his dilemma, the leper completely put his pride aside, and found himself **kneeling** down to Jesus. You see, once we acknowledge the healing potential of Jesus' hands, and **beseech** or seek Him out, we then must be willing to adopt an appropriate posture of humility. When we find Him, and are brought face to face with our own unworthiness to receive the miracle we seek, we ought to join the leper in kneeling before this Great Physician. How often have we lost our opportunity to be healed, to be liberated from the bondage of disease, because our pride inhibited or utterly prohibited us from humble obedience to the Lord? Yet, the leper had neither doubt nor misgivings about displaying a welcomed subservience to the Master's power and authority, for Jesus was his only hope.

But in addition to **seeking** the Lord, and **kneeling** before Him, the leper amazingly began **saying**; he began to speak to Jesus. Understand, it had taken a major leap of faith for the brother just to entertain the thought of being clean! Living in some forlorn nook and cranny in the outcast society of lepers, he hadn't even allowed himself the luxury of the thought, before he heard of Jesus! Because of his psychological need to be reconciled to his new, despicable lot in life, he'd managed to put even the thought of ever being healed out of his mind. It seemed so implausible, so impossible. Therefore, to even think the thought, or to mentally craft the words, much less to actually apply breath to those words — took extraordinary resolve. Like many of us confronted with similar situations of apparent hopelessness, the leper could've gotten cold feet! Far too often we don't want to sound silly; we don't want to look foolish; we don't want to seem irrational — asking for a healing! What if the healing doesn't become manifest? What will people say? Aren't we just exhibiting denial? Shouldn't we simply get on with our debilitated lives?

Indeed, we can retreat into the apparent certainty of our sickness, or we can stand on God's Word that affirms that nothing is too hard for God; that although with man some things are impossible, with God all things are possible; that too often we have not, simply because we ask not! Just think how blessed we are to have at our disposal today the entire weight and testimony of scripture, which gives us the authority to believe God for our healing. Perhaps all that was available to that desperate leper was the knowledge that there was a stranger in town whose reputation had preceded Him. For the leper, however, that was enough; for Jesus was his only hope.

So he summoned up the determination, the fortitude, the courage to form his lips and to open his mouth, saying, "If thou wilt … if you want to … if you choose to … you can make me clean!"

Well, Church, as we keep reading this passage, we discover what happens when one seeks out, kneels before, and speaks to Jesus about our conditions. A spiritual, sequential, therapeutic regimen is initiated!

First, Jesus moves with compassion. Like the writer of Hebrews, I'm so grateful that "we have not a high priest who cannot be touched with the feeling of our infirmities." He's been there, He knows, and He feels for us. Second, Jesus does the "Ma Bell"; He reaches out and touches us!

True enough, in the case of this leper, Jesus moved with compassion, put forth His hand and touched him. But as wonderful as it was for this outcast to feel loved — for the offensive disease made lepers almost unlovable — that wasn't the reason he'd come to Jesus. What the leper really wanted was to be healed! As rare and as special as it was for this untouchable to be touched — and nobody ever touched lepers — that brother wanted to be healed!

So, thank God, the third step in the therapeutic sequence transpired; Jesus began to talk back! Church, if we want to be healed, we've got to learn that in the process of **seeking**, **kneeling** and **praying**, we must be willing to become engaged in a two-way conversation — a dialogue! Our supplications, our petitions are not about monologue. Listen as the Lord spoke to the leper — "You said to me, 'If you wanted to ... ' Well, I want to! Be thou clean!" And the therapeutic intervention worked! "As soon ... " If only to record his point more emphatically and unequivocally, the writer reiterates, "immediately, the leprosy departed from him, and he was cleansed!"

In follow-up of the healing, Jesus made only a single request of this man, now with a miraculous, new lease on a life of health and wholeness. The Lord clearly, explicitly instructed the brother <u>not</u> to tell anything about what had happened to him to anybody. He was simply to go back to the public health "physician" — to the infectious disease specialist of the day, who again would employ the guidelines and the authority to declare him either "clean" or "unclean" — and present himself for examination. "Go thy way and shew thyself to the priest." Do exactly what the doc tells you! Follow the Law.

Sacrifice the lambs and the dove. Bring the birds, cedarwood, scarlet, and hyssop. Let the priest put a dab of oil on your right ear, your thumb, your big toe! The world will then know that you're now "clean!" **"Just don't tell anybody ... "**

I'm positive that the once hopeless brother must have gratefully said in his heart, "Certainly, Jesus. Anything you say, Master. Sure, my Lord. I won't tell **nobody**!" I believe he had every intention of complying with Jesus' request. He wasn't lying; in his heart, he meant what he said!

But "as he went out," something happened! I'm not sure what it was; the Word doesn't really say. I can only assume that the brother was struck by several, notable observations.

Perhaps he happened upon a puddle, and for the first time got a good look at his transformed, non-leprous face — the same face that had been covered for so long, pockmarked by eroded flesh and a collapsed nose. Something inside of him began to swell up,

"My, my, my! I **said I wasn't gonna tell nobody**, but! ... "

Perhaps he noticed that he could now see out of his right eye that had been sightless for a long time, secondary to a leprous corneal ulcer ... and he felt like bursting out, **"said I wasn't gonna tell nobody**, but! ..."

Perhaps he looked at his now-nimble hand, that had been hideously withered ... and his heart began to pound, **"said I wasn't gonna tell nobody**, but ! ..."

Perhaps, as he walked, he began to realize that the incapacitating pain in his forearm and leg, an ever-present legacy of leprous neuropathy, was gone ... **"said I wasn't gonna tell nobody, but! ..."**

Perhaps he allowed himself to boldly do what a short time before was unthinkable — to check out his own skin, which to his amazement now felt just like a baby's ... and he almost shouted out: **"said I wasn't gonna tell nobody**, but! ..."

Perhaps he began to reminisce about and reflect upon how long he'd been exiled to that leper colony; how long he'd had to hide in "good company"; how long he'd been required to ring out "unclean, unclean" whenever he came close to non-lepers ... he felt like now ringing out, **"said I wasn't gonna tell nobody**, but! ..."

But perhaps, it was as he got closer to the village — and started thinking about how he'd be able to hug his momma, and his wife, and his children again — that he could no longer contain himself! Perhaps it was then that he got an incurable case of the "can't-help-its," and the Bible said he began to "publish it much, and to blaze abroad the matter!"

It's not recorded; there's no transcript, but I can almost hear that one-time leper in the words of those old traditional, Christian joy songs:

> I looked at my hands, and they looked new,
> I looked at my feet, and they did, too!..

You oughta been there ... **said I wasn't gonna tell nobody,**

BUT ... I COULDN'T KEEP IT TO MYSELF —
WHAT THE LORD HAS DONE FOR ME!

Can I get a witness? Somebody's bursting at the seams with gratitude to the Lord today, knowing exactly how that brother must have felt! When I, personally, "think about the goodness of Jesus, and all that He's done for me, my soul cries out, '**said I wasn't gonna tell nobody,** but! ... '"

Truly, whatever the problem, whatever the situation, whatever the condition, whatever the disease ... try seeking Jesus, try kneeling before Him, try speaking unto the Lord your heart's desire. I assure you that — as you go, just like the leper — you will experience your own healing, by whatever means, and in whatever form Jesus prescribes it and delivers it. You, too, may end up shouting, **"said I wasn't gonna tell nobody,** but! ... "

THE THERAPEUTIC SIDE OF JUDAISM

Micah D. Greenstein

<u>The Prince of Tides</u> was a movie my wife and I had been looking forward to seeing for some time. What we didn't expect to see, though, was a packed hall of congregants. There were so many Jews in attendance, Federation would have done very well to pass the plate around at the theater!

<u>The Prince of Tides</u>, as many of you may already know, is based on Pat Conroy's book about the relationships and traumas of a Southern family in Beaufort, South Carolina. When the daughter of the family is saved from a suicide attempt in New York City, her Jewish psychiatrist, Dr. Lowenstein, summons the younger brother to Manhattan to help uncover what may have triggered his sister's depression. The movie raises a host of issues. However, one of the most powerful messages it conveys is the importance of expressing one's inner self. And while few of us have endured the traumas experienced by the characters in <u>The Prince of Tides</u>, I think all of us can relate to painful memories from our own past, as well as other obstacles that have hindered our spiritual growth and development. As the counseling sessions unfold in <u>The Prince of Tides</u>, the brother gradually experiences the healing power of grieving, which enables him to

love again and feel again. The movie isn't so much a pitch for psychotherapy as it is about self–discovery, trust, holding onto pleasant memories, and letting go of painful ones.

Upon returning home from the movie and heading to my study for some temple-related work, it occurred to me that Judaism and The Prince of Tides are connected in significant and important ways — and not just because the psychiatrist in the movie and producer-director happens to be a Jewish girl from Brooklyn named Barbra Streisand! For me, the underlying message of The Prince of Tides is a very Jewish one, and it is that message I wish to explore with you on this Shabbat.

Ask 10 Jews to define Judaism and you'll probably get 10 different answers. One person might respond that Judaism is simply a religion in contrast to other religions. Another individual might describe Judaism in theological terms as an eternal covenant, a binding and sacred agreement between God and the Jewish people to take care of God's world and each other. A third individual might view Judaism in less lofty terms and identify Judaism in terms of attachment to the Jewish people and to the cultural life of the Jew.

Still others may view Judaism as a treasure-chest of learning and scholarship, a library of wisdom, literature, history, art, music, and philosophy. Young children tend to perceive Judaism more as a series of rituals, stories, and holiday observances than as a thinking man's faith.

I'd like to suggest another perspective on the meaning and purpose of Judaism, based in part on my experience as a practicing Jew and triggered also by the psychological themes dealt with in The Prince of Tides. I'd like to suggest that Judaism may also be conceived as an attempt to make meaning and order out of the disorder surrounding our private and public lives. Judaism provides answers to questions like "What is our purpose on earth?" "How can we sanctify life and lend meaning to our existence?" "Why be good?" "What are our obligations to our families, friends, and community?" "How can I be my best and set my priorities straight?" "How can I overcome the tragedies and rough moments that have made life so difficult to live at times?" Seen in this light, Judaism is therapy for the living. I use the term therapy not in a clinical sense, but in a spiritual and curative sense. Judaism, when properly and consistently applied, serves to heal and make whole instead of concerning itself with **saving** souls, as some faiths do. Judaism devotes itself in large part to **healing** souls.

I think most of us can relate to the spiritual healing power of Judaism. Ask frequent temple-goers why they attend services on a regular basis, and they are likely to speak of how this hour of worship brings them a sense of inner serenity and reflection. One congregant told me that his favorite minute of the week is the silent meditation during Shabbat services, because it's the only uninterrupted moment of silence in his entire week!

I would explain Judaism's curative potential in terms of three main ingredients: our tradition's inherent optimism, its respect for pain, and its approach to spiritual growth as an ongoing process rather than as a one-time experience.

To demonstrate Judaism's optimistic outlook, consider the Book of Exodus from which we have been reading in recent weeks. Isn't it curious that God found His people among the downtrodden and humiliated Hebrew slaves of Egypt? What a sorry group those slaves were in Pharaoh's day! And yet, from these slaves arose our ancestors. They became a new light for the world and the source for some of the most honored and civilized ideals in the history of humankind. The moral of this Exodus story seems to be that it is not what an individual is **today** that is all-important, but what a person can potentially become **tomorrow**. A person may have been bad yesterday and feel trapped today, but our tradition teaches that he can always choose goodness and tap into the spark of divinity within his nature. The promise of a better tomorrow no matter what our past has been is at the heart of Judaism and the Jewish experience through the ages. (It is also the way in which we end every

Sabbath evening service.)

Judaism also teaches that life is a series of adjustments, sometimes painful ones; at certain junctures in our lives, we must come to grips with the loss of loved ones, the loss of certain hopes, and the loss of our physical abilities. In short, we have to come to terms with the limits of life. But life is not just about adjusting to limits. Life is also about seeking purpose. We are, by nature, purpose-seeking creatures. We want our lives to have meaning and purpose. We want our lives to count for something. We want to help people. We want to contribute to life-enhancing causes. We want to help preserve the Jewish people and ensure the future of Judaism. We want, in some small way, to fulfill the task God has set for us, for deep down, we know that we are here for a purpose.

But what about when, in the words of our prayerbook, "doubt troubles us and pain clouds the mind?" Our tradition teaches that at times like these we must not be afraid to express our sorrow. Unlike other faith systems, Judaism does not promise us miraculous consolation. But our tradition does teach the aching heart how to express its pain in love and respect without denying the tragedy itself. Whether that tragedy be a personal setback, an assault on our well-being, or the loss of a loved one, Judaism offers wonderful coping strategies when living hurts. I often marvel at the emotional and psychological insights of the Rabbis who recognized the need not only to support grievers, but to have respect for the pain, anger and disorientation that often accompany the grieving process. Judaism helps mend grief-stricken hearts one step at a time, so that slowly and gradually, we find a way to live with our losses.

It is no accident, for instance, that Judaism prescribes three stages in the mourning process. Our tradition summons us to face the tragedies that befall us squarely and honestly. The wording of the beloved twenty-third Psalm supports this view. You will note that our Bible reads, "Yea though I **walk** through the valley of the shadow of death." It doesn't say that we can fly over the valley, detour around it, or run through it. We have to walk, one step at a time.

Perhaps the most touching scene in the movie <u>The Prince of Tides</u> is when the central character reunites with his sister after her failed suicide attempt. In this poignant and emotional scene, we cry with the brother and sister for what they've been through, and yet, we rejoice that both have walked through the valley of the shadow they have experienced. The valley each of us must go through is open on both sides. The Rabbis teach that it need not be a permanent dwelling-place. We can somehow walk through it and sanctify life again in spite of our loss.

A simple farmer was asked by a visitor from the city during a torrential rainstorm whether he thought it would stop raining. The farmer answered dryly, "It usually does." Like nature, we can heal ourselves even though the losses we experience may always remain with us. And Jewish living through worship, study and deeds can help restore an individual's hopeful and healthful attitude toward life itself.

Rabbis are not psychologists and psychologists are not Rabbis, and yet our tradition offers spiritual resources to make us whole and complete, no matter what stage or condition we may be in. Judaism is more than a religion; it's also a prescription for healthy living and peace of mind. When we consider the reality that God is with and in us, when we allow ourselves to express our grief, and when we keep our recovery expectations reasonable and live our lives one step at a time, we can turn our tears into dreams and achieve our highest hopes.

I think this is what the Rabbis of the Talmud were aiming for when they wrote this prayer.

> May you live to see your world fulfilled.
> May your eyes shine with the light of holy words
> And your face reflect the brightness of the heavens.
> May your heart be filled with intuition
> And your words be filled with insight ...

May songs of praise be upon your tongue
And your vision straight before you.
(Bavli, Berachot 17A)

Like the character in <u>The Prince of Tides</u>, may each of us
increase our self-knowledge. May we learn to uncover whatever
may be standing in the way of our spiritual development and ful-
fillment, so that unencumbered by old fears and guilts, we can
return home freer and happier than ever before. May we discover the spiritual resources within us to improve ourselves, our
relationships, and the world around us. And may we also come
to know how Jewish living and Jewish learning can help us in
our common striving for Shalom — wholeness, completeness,
healing and peace.

HEALING THE WOUNDS OF THE HEART

Text: Isaiah 61:1   Brooks Ramsey

*H*e has sent me to bind up the broken-hearted.
(Isaiah 61:1)

I have no desire to be morbid, but reality forces me to believe that underneath all human experience stands the presence of pain. Pathos is always with us. There is the possibility that pain may be the ultimate source of all other negative feelings. We become angry, depressed, or filled with anxiety because we are hurting. In fact, one school of psychotherapy is dedicated to helping find and face what it calls the "primal pain" — the pain of early childhood that lies beneath all subsequent pain.

Human pain has its source in many experiences. Some of it is related to physical suffering. Illness can take a devastating toll on us. For 10 years, I witnessed the excruciating pain endured by my wife. Arthritis destroyed the cartilage in both hips. Hardly able to take a step, she was headed inevitably for a wheel-chair. Until, thank God, the skills of a surgeon and the medical community were able to provide total hip replacements. Now, four months later, she (the Bionic Woman) is able to walk unaided without pain. This gloriously underscores my belief that pain and suffering are not the will of God. The Divine will is for all suffering to be ended. In my view, the only suffering that is of value is the suffering to end suffering.

But the pain that afflicts us the most is the inner suffering that pierces our hearts. Sometimes it is the pain of grief at the loss of someone we love deeply — by death, divorce or geographical removal. Can we not feel the poignancy of the words of W.H. Auden, who wrote after the death of his beloved friend,

> Stop all the clocks, cut off the telephone,
> Prevent the dog from barking with a juicy bone,
> Silence the pianos and with muffled drum
> Bring in the coffin, let the mourners come.
> He was my North, my South, my East and West.
> My working day and my Sunday rest.
> My noon, my midnight, my talk, my song.
> I thought love would last forever: I was wrong.

Crushed hopes also bring the pain of disappointment. Discovering the limitations of life, we suffer the regrets of what might have been. We push on dauntlessly perhaps, but cannot escape the feeling that we have not attained all that could have been done. Life has not always turned out like we wanted it to.

Then again, there are the wounds that come from misunderstanding. Someone we counted on has failed to support us in our hour of need. The pain of betrayal hurts the worst of all. The deepest pain to the ancient prophet was, "I was wounded in the house of my friend" (Zechariah 13:6).

A woman crushed with disappointment said it most poignantly in my office recently: "I feel like someone has taken a big splinter and driven it right to the core of my heart." Who among us cannot identify with that expression of personal pain? When have you last felt pain like that?

The Apostle Paul spoke of "thorn in the flesh." He would have understood what the woman was going through.

A splinter in the heart — or a thorn in the flesh — they both say the same thing. We human beings are at times subjected to a pain so piercing that it can only be adequately described as a "heart wound."

It is in this context of human struggle that Jesus stood up in the synagogue and read from the prophet Isaiah the words, "He has sent me to bind up the brokenhearted" (Isaiah 61:1). He enunciated His message and ministry as being one of hope and healing. He brought healing to bodies, to be sure, but His deeper healing was for the wounds of the heart. The method He chose for doing this is made clear in His ministry to persons. How He ministered to the brokenhearted is still God's method today for penetrating our deepest need with love and power.

Here are some ways healing takes place:

THE AFFIRMATION OF LIFE

Jesus declared, "I came that they may have life and have it abundantly" (John 10:10). In our struggle against destructive forces, we are urged to stand up and affirm our determination to live triumphantly. Paul Tillich, the eminent theologian, emphasized that we are always threatened with "Non-Being." By that, he meant our lives are judged as worth nothing. We are nobodies. We don't count. Tillich urges us to that highest form of courage — to deny "Non-Being," and affirm our "Being." In spite of assaults on our inner spirits, we can determine that we will commit ourselves to the kind of life Jesus referred to as "abundant."

A few nights ago, I listed to a CD of Messiaen's moving Quartet for the End of Time. He wrote it while imprisoned by the Nazis in World War II. Confined to a stalag with barely enough food and no heat, he committed himself to write a piece of music that would express his belief that evil would not have the last word. He wrote it for the only four musical instruments available in the camp — a broken-down piano, a clarinet that could hardly be played, a violin and cello of the cheapest variety.

On a freezing night in January 1944, the musicians played his composition. Present in the mess hall were the disheveled prisoners of war and their German guards. They listened to music so gorgeous that even their guards wept. To hear the music now gives one a surge of faith. The last movement is a piano and violin duet that Messiaen entitled, "Praise for the Immortality of Jesus." It was an ennobling witness to his belief that life would have the last word in the struggle against the death forces.

We have been given another source:

A SENSE OF DIGNITY

I like the word "dignity." It has nothing to do with stiffness or snobbishness. It speaks more of self-respect and honor. The source of such high virtues is one's understanding that the essence of our being comes because of God's creative act. A coffee mug that I keep for special days has written on it, "I was born entitled." It reminds me that my privileges of personhood were not conferred on me by any other human being or any human institution. They came because I am a child of God.

It seems to me that the whole ministry of Jesus was dedicated to raising persons to this high sense of personal dignity. He saw beyond the situation they were in to the essential person they were. He saw also potential — what they could become. To Simon Peter, he affirmed, "You are Simon, you will become Peter"(John 1:42). From a crude fisherman to the Rock (the meaning of the name Peter) of the church. What a transformation! Can you imagine what that did to enhance Peter's sense of divine entitlement?

A number of years ago, I spent a month in the country of Panama. While there, I discovered San Miguelito, a community that had been miraculously transformed by the Gospel message. Once, it had existed as the most abject and poverty-ridden part of Panama. When I visited it, it had become a beautiful community where flowers grew and children played in security and peace. In the midst was a medical clinic, a school and a church. Four priests and five nuns from Chicago had come and established a church through which a message of hope and love had begun the process of transformation. I asked Father Leo Mahan what they had done. He said, "We went out and visited the people and told them that they were the Sons and Daughters of God, and as such, were the leaders of humanity." Then he said to me, "They believed us and began to act that way."

That kind of endowment of dignity moves persons out of mud-floored houses to permanent housing where flowers do grow and children play joyfully.

In the midst of our adversities, we can claim our full worth as sons and daughters of God. When we do this, we find a marvelous resource for facing life's challenges triumphantly. When pain punctures the heart, we can keep our heads high with a strong determination to express the full nobility of our personhood.

AN ENDUREMENT OF POWER

No matter what the circumstances, we are never without available power. In every situation, there is a saving possibility. We have been given the resources to stand against every destructive force that hurls itself against us. Defeat comes only when we fail to utilize the strength that lies within us.

The words of Christ speak loudly, "In this world you have tribulation, but be of good cheer: I have overcome the world" (John 16:33). The word "tribulation" has as its root meaning, "grinding." That is pain at its deepest level, to be ground as powder by the tragic events of life. But we can never be ground into nothingness if we connect with the power of Him who said, "I have overcome the world."

An old Scottish minister said it this way, "Peace does not

come with the absence of trouble, but with the conscious realization of adequate resources."

On a recent birthday of mine, I received a heart-warming letter from one of my children. He pointed out that I had reached the "philosophical age of reflection." Then he gave me truth to reflect on. It was about the struggle of life forces and death forces. I share with you his philosophical insights:

> What I see is a slender thread of continuity of life, of experience. Slender because it implies time and time eludes us — it is beyond comprehension. But the thread is also of absolute strength because it can and does hold fast individual universes of experience which this world tries every day, every hour to break apart, but fails to do so because it (this world) is the victim of true power.

These profound words spoke to me eloquently that in the midst of forces that would break me apart, there stands an absolute power that sustains me, and will not let the threat of spiritual significance be broken.

Of course, we all have access to this power of faith. To believe that God is with us and that the divine presence will never leave us, gives us courage to go on in spite of the most agonizing experiences of life.

To affirm life, to claim our sense of dignity and to open ourselves to that absolute power of faith is to experience healing at its deepest level.

LEARNING HOW TO LIVE WITH A LIMP

Text: II Corinthians 12:7–9   Benjamin Lawson Hooks

And lest I should be exalted above measure through the abundance of the revelations, there was given to me a thorn in the flesh, the messenger of Satan to buffet me, lest I should be exalted above measure. For this thing I besought the Lord thrice, that it might depart from me. And he said unto me, "My grace is sufficient for thee: for my strength is made perfect in weakness."

(II Corinthians 12:7–9)

There are many definitions for the word limp: stagger, fumble, hobble, shuffle, flop, languish. There are also many ways to have a limp. I am not speaking only about physical limps, but also about social, psychological, moral limps. Times when we fail. Those things in our life that we would like to see changed. In other words, one way or another all of us have a limp. **All of us have a limp**.

It may be that you have a mother or father who is not really acting like a mother or father, or you may have a husband or wife who is unfaithful or unkind or not generous. You may have a son or daughter who doesn't act like a child ought to act. You may have a problem on your job, and I remind you, that the longer you have been on your job, the less time you have to serve. Some of us have limps we picked up — limps we acquired, habits and problems we could and should throw off. There are those who have an alcoholic limp. Many people are going to the gambling hall with a strike-it-rich limp. They feel if they get to the casino, everything is going to be all right. They have the one-armed bandit limp — the dazzling lights of the slot machine have made a lot of people limp. Then again, we can have a limp of the mind, where one fails to believe in him or herself. You feel like you haven't ever been anybody, and won't ever be anybody. You have an inferiority complex limp. If you think that way, you're going to be that way. Many of us have a go-slow limp. You say to me, "Reverend, don't put me on anything. I'm just a bench member." We have the bench member limp. We don't want to be called on to do anything, "just leave me alone."

Then we have the limp of people who tell you that "I've tried." They say, "Reverend, I tried to push myself from the table"; they have the fried chicken, too much cake and rich food limp. I had it too. I tell you, hear me today, all of us have some kind of problem. If you don't see your problems, you know someone in your family who has a problem and sometimes the phone rings, and you hear about someone in trouble. I find it amusing how such little things cause most of the trouble. I was in an elevator the other day listening to someone tell about a cousin arguing over $20.00, and he ended up getting stabbed to death. When that happens, then we have the gossip limp. Those of us who like to tell it and those who like to hear it. If we don't have clacking tongues, we have itching ears.

In this passage we have selected today, Paul, the Great Apostle, talks about his limp, his problem. The scholars who have examined this passage are in disagreement as to what type of thorn in the flesh Paul suffered from — whether it was physical or mental. Some suggest it was epileptic seizures. Others say he was approaching blindness; others say he had crippling arthritis, but whatever the problem, Paul spells out clearly that he wished to be relieved from it. He cries out to the Lord three times for relief. He wanted to be cleansed, healed, cured, relieved. Paul then explains that God did not heal, cure or remove, but instead says to him, "My Grace is sufficient for thee. I can cause you to live abundantly, fully, completely, victoriously with the thorns in your flesh. You do all things necessary for my kingdom, but you will keep your problem — my grace is sufficient for thee."

Let me make it clear, there are some problems that with God's help we should and can overcome — but if you have a thorn in the flesh, a handicap or limp, if you please — God's strength is made perfect in weakness.

What I would suggest is you can learn to live with a limp or handicap, and still serve God well.

I heard Dr. William Holmes Borders of Atlanta tell about a man who had a limp. His limp was that he couldn't read or write. This man was the janitor of the bank. One day one of the vice presidents called him to tell him he was going to make him head janitor. He told the man to fill out the application. The janitor looked at him and said, "I am sorry, but I cannot read or write."

The young vice president said, "You're here in my bank and can't read or write? I am not only not going to promote you, but you can't work here, you cannot have the job you've got." So, he lost his job because he couldn't read or write.

Dr. Borders said the man went and got a wagon, and started gathering junk, old things, collecting what other people didn't want. (Young people don't know anything about that line of work. We used to have men who collected old junk, collected bottles, rags, iron and then sold it for what they could get.) About 20 years later, this same man walked back into the bank. This time he came to deposit more than $100,000. He first, however, wanted some financial advice. Well, he had so much money, they let him see the president. The president said, "I'm so glad to see you." The president was the same man who had fired him because he couldn't read or write. As they were talking, it dawned on the president who this man was, and he said, "Oh Charlie, just think what you could have done if you had been able to read and write."

He said, "I guess I'd still be the head janitor at the bank." Every now and then, you've got to take a handicap and make it a stepping stone. **Hear me today!**

Young people who are making excuses and talking about dope, I want you to listen to me. Yes, they make dope, but you don't have to take it. Yes, they have gangs, but you don't have to join them. Yes, they have pistols, but you don't have to use them. Somehow you've got to make a handicap a stepping stone.

Look at Fannie Crosby. She was blind, but one day a woman said, "Fannie, I's so sorry that you cannot see."

Fannie Crosby said, "But blessed assurance, Jesus is mine, Oh what a foretaste of glory divine. Heir of salvation, purchase of God, I've been born of His spirit. I've been washed in His blood. I may not see down here, but thank God I will see over there" ("Blessed Assurance").

When I had my heart operation that Saturday morning, they cut me open, broke my breastbone, took my heart, and changed it around. I was almost dead. Since I have been out of the hospital, there are a lot of things I used to take for granted — things I can't do now. If I try to pick up a suitcase, I am going to fall with the suitcase. I cannot run; I cannot eat like I used to. I can't talk like I used to. I can't stay up like I used to. I have a limp now. But I want to tell you something: I am learning how to live with it. Yes, I am, and I thank God that I know you can live with a limp and still claim victory. "Oh how I love Jesus. Oh how I love Jesus, because He first loved me. There is a name I love to hear. I love to sing its worth. It sounds like music to my ears, it's the sweetest name on earth" ("Oh, How I Love Jesus," Frederick Whitfield).

Remember, His grace is sufficient for thee.

Paul became the greatest preacher of his time; he overcame the thorns in his flesh — **SO CAN WE ALL!**

FROM BROKENNESS TO WHOLENESS

Text: Matthew 4:23–25   Louise Upchurch Lawson

*O*ne of the most striking and unmistakable characteristics of Jesus' ministry was his ability to heal the sick. Jesus' power to heal cut across every dimension of human experience, as he could heal the body, mind and soul. This morning's Scripture lesson puts it succinctly:

> So Jesus' fame spread throughout all Syria, and they brought to him all the sick, those who were afflicted with various diseases and pains, demoniacs, epileptics and paralytics, and Jesus cured them.
>
> (Matthew 4:24)

It's no wonder then, that down through the ages Jesus has been referred to as the Great Physician, because crowds literally followed him everywhere, hoping for miraculous cures.

That such a significant part of Jesus' God-given ministry was devoted to healing tells us something crucial about the nature of God. That there was and is such a great deal of healing to be done in the first place tells us something crucial about the nature of humanity. What I would like for us to explore are our own expectations of God through Christ in this area of healing. When it comes to sickness, disease and cure, the key question for most Christians seems to be, "What role does God play in my illness and/or recovery?"

I want us to look at the hardest part of that question first: What role does God play in my illness? This question demands a responsible answer, because your whole theology (your view of who God is) is ultimately derived from your answer to this question. Let me show you what I mean.

There are Christians who believe that if you or I get cancer, then God has sent it. In other words, God hand-picks people out of a crowd to experience a particular illness. How does a Christian person arrive at this conclusion? Usually from deductive reasoning, working backwards. The sequence goes something like this:

1) God is sovereign.
2) That means that God is in control of everything that happens in this world.
3) Furthermore, everything that God does happens for a reason.
4) Therefore, if I get cancer, then it is because God has willed it as part of God's divine plan.

It's easy to see how this conclusion can be drawn. But what one is left with as a result is a God who wills disease, brokenness and death on humankind. And not only does God will this type of destruction, God "sends" it. This notion of God has God spending lots of time and energy involved in what we usually call evil.

Now, let's get really analytical here. What's wrong with this picture of God? There are two things principally wrong with it:

The first is that sin is absent in this picture of reality. Let's redo the logic sequence taking sin into account. It goes like this:

1) God **is** most certainly sovereign.

2) God has a will and a plan for all humans and all humanity.

3) But that will and plan is for the **redemption** of humanity — not its destruction.

God, Scripture tells us, is eternally at work to bring health, not sickness; to bring wholeness from brokenness; to restore what has been torn down; to rehabilitate those who are wounded; in a word, to redeem, transform, and re-create a fallen and broken humanity.

The very nature of God is at stake here. Either God fundamentally does, works and wills health, salvation, and wholeness and all that is good, **OR** we have a God who can participate in evil itself.

The second thing that is wrong with the notion that if I am sick, then it must be God's will is that everything that happens in this world is NOT God's will. Just because something happens does not make whatever happens God's will. Think about this for a moment. Children starve, people kill each other, violence ruins human life each day ... are these things God's will? They can't be. What Scripture tells us from Genesis to Revelation is that our world is permeated with sin. We live in a fallen world, we are people who sin, and sin is a real power that contradicts the purposes of God. Sin twists and distorts the good gifts that God gives us. Sin tears down people, places and things. Sin works towards deterioration, destruction and ruin. We see the effects of sin each and every day. Saying that whatever comes to pass is the will of God ignores the power and presence of sin as a force in this world of ours — and ignoring sin ignores the Biblical witness altogether. What we can say about God's role in disease and sickness is that God is in the business of bringing good out of evil, of bringing hope where there is only despair, of healing, even where there may be no cure. In other words, the presence of sickness does not mean the absence of God. Nor does it mean the absence of faith. It only means that we are human and vulnerable to those things that attack body, mind and soul. So ... do I believe that God sends disease? NO. But do I believe that God can use any human misfortune in order to draw us closer to Him? ABSOLUTELY!

This past week, a colleague from Mississippi called me on the phone to ask a favor. I hadn't seen or heard from him in almost 15 years. As we were catching up, he told me that about two months ago he had a seizure. He blacked out and woke up in the Intensive Care Unit of his local hospital.

He is in his early forties, so he was shocked. He has no family history of epilepsy or seizures of any sort. He confessed to me that this physical disability has caused him to do some hard thinking about God, his family, his career, his hopes and dreams, and generally what's important in life. He said, "I haven't been able to drive for the last eight weeks. Do you have any idea how a type A personality reacts to inactivity and dependence?"

"I think I can guess," I said.

"Well, I'll tell you this," he said. "I discovered that my wife can drive a car just as well as I can; that my children love me not for what I can do but for who I am — and that's a little humbling; and that the church runs quite well without me too — that God can still use even the new me, not just the old me." He said, "The most meaningful verse for me in Scripture has been Psalm 46:10, 'Be still and know that I am God.' I was never still before; now I know like I have never known, and trust like I have never trusted."

What I was hearing from my friend was what I call "healing." There has been no cure. His condition has not reversed so that he is like he formerly was. That's what a cure is. But I submit to you that God has been at work in his life, building up, mending, healing, encouraging, strengthening him body, mind, and spirit. You see, just because there is no "cure" does not mean there has been no healing.

Time to address the second part of the perennial question

that we started with: "What role does God have in my recovery?" That depends. Sometimes God cures. I have known people and you have, too, who miraculously recover from serious illness and injury "for no apparent reason." In certain instances, God cures outright. How, who, and why, I don't know. God knows. But to decide that because there has been no miraculous cure — that God is absent or has deliberately forsaken us — is erroneous thinking. It doesn't allow for the healing that my friend experienced. There are people who are physically very ill, whose illness does not affect their being at all. They remain interested in other people, do not focus on or complain about their own condition, and actually pray for and encourage others. What a testimony to the healing power of God to be at work despite physical infirmity! The converse can be true as well. There are people who are sick in mind or spirit and in perfect health otherwise. They need healing just as badly as their counterparts who suffer physically.

What we know about God's will is revealed most fully and perfectly in the life and ministry of Jesus Christ. And what we know about the activity of Jesus Christ is that he spent a great deal of time healing those who were ill in body, mind, or soul. It is therefore safe to assume that God wills physical health, emotional health and spiritual health. It is therefore safe to assume that God is at work bringing health, wholeness, and healing to broken and sick humanity. Having said this, we need to be frank about what we can expect from God in this regard. God never promised that if we would only believe, then we would be free of sickness and other ills. God never said that Christians are a favored few in whom God would work miraculous cures on demand. God never said that on this side of heaven, believers were promised a life free of trial, difficulty, pain, or frailty.

But listen to what God has promised. God has promised to be with us always, even to the end of the age. God is not a fair-weather deity who vanishes when the first sign of trouble hits. God has promised that if we will only trust in Him in this life, then though our bodies fail, we will not die — we will go <u>from life to life</u>. God has promised that no matter what our physical condition in this world, in the next there will be, "no more death, neither sorrow, nor crying, neither shall there be any more pain: for the former things are passed away."

Whereas God occasionally cures in this world, God's cure-rate in the coming kingdom is 100%! We pray for a cure in the present, and there is nothing wrong with that. But let's not in our desire for a cure overlook God's power in healing. Let's be honest, healing is slow and gradual, when what we want from God is immediate, overnight results (just like FedEx ... when it absolutely, positively has to be there in the morning). But healing is every bit as much the work of God as a cure, and God has always done some of His best work slowly.

Don't just ask for a cure, remember to ask for healing. And if you are sick, don't just look for a cure, examine yourself to see what God is doing in your life to heal your attitudes, not just your body; your relationships, not just your condition; your devotional and prayer life, not just your physique. Ask yourself, "How is God using this time of illness in my life?" Generally you will either get better or get bitter.

May we all, when confronted with illness of any kind, learn as my friend did, to "be still and know that God is God." **AMEN.**

THE DIVINE DESIGN FOR GOOD HEALTH

Kenneth P. Story

$\mathcal{S}$ome sort of National Health Care Program is on the horizon. The debate about National Health Care is vigorous and caustic for at least three reasons:

1. Most Americans will be affected directly by any kind of National Health Care Program;
2. Knowing how our government typically operates, there is real concern that the quality of medical care will decline; and (for the same reason),
3. There is a good chance the cost of medical care will increase for most Americans.

Well, let me tell you there is another Health Care Plan that has not yet been mentioned by the politicians or press. It is the most effective and most universally applicable health care program the world has ever seen, and it is the least expensive. I am calling it the **Divine Design for Good Health**.

John writes to some friends in his third New Testament

letter saying, "Beloved, I wish above all things that thou mayest prosper and be in health even as thy soul prospereth." Why do you suppose John included this statement in a letter that dealt with spiritual issues? Upon what did John base his hope for his friends' wellness and wholeness in life?

The answer is that John knew the Lord and His Word well enough to understand that God wants His people to be blessed in many ways (including enjoyment of our maximum potential for good health). Our health must be of considerable importance to the Lord because He included so much information in the Bible about it.

MAINTAINING PHYSICAL HEALTH (EXODUS 15:26)

When the subject of "health" is mentioned, we probably think first about physical health. The Bible gives us some very helpful instructions about maintaining physical health. Turn to Exodus 15:26.

HISTORY

This verse was written about 3,400 years ago. At that time Egypt was the dominant world power, and Egypt's medical science was considered the best on earth. In 1552 B.C., the Egyptians produced a medical textbook called Papyrus Ebers that contained the latest medical knowledge of that day. It offered treatments that seem curious to us today.

Papyrus Ebers advised physicians to treat snake bites by giving the victims "magic water," water poured over an Egyptian idol, to drink. If a splinter was embedded in your skin, the textbook advised applying a mixture of worm's blood and donkey dung. That mix would be full of germs including tetanus so the treatment was likely to result in lockjaw.

Papyrus Ebers even included a prescription for baldness, which was a mixture of fat from six different animals plus a donkey tooth crushed in honey. It doesn't work. In most instances, the prescriptions given in Papyrus Ebers were more harmful to a patient than his original health problem — but that was the most advanced medical science in 1152 B.C.

About the time that this ancient medical textbook was written, God was calling Moses to lead the three million Hebrew slaves out from under Egyptian bondage. Along with that call to freedom and destiny, God said to Moses, "I am going to give you some prescriptions that will keep the people healthy."

DO YOU RECALL SOME OF GOD'S PRESCRIPTIONS?

God said, "Don't eat animal fat" (Leviticus 7:22–24). Now doesn't that sound modern? How did Moses know 3,500 years ago that animal fat is a primary source of harmful cholesterol in our diet? God told him so. God also told them, "Don't eat certain foods." We understand that some of those foods — pork — would have been treacherous when prepared under the primitive conditions of those days and also difficult to digest. According to God's instructions, food was to be well-cooked. The Bible even talks about the problem of overeating. God does not mind meddling. These and other divinely revealed directions about eating protected God's people from diseases and illnesses such as trichinosis, arteriosclerosis, and heart disease.

We know today that infections can be spread through contact with blood. God knew that 3,500 years ago, and He instructed His people to scrupulously avoid contact with blood, animal or human. After any contact with blood, a person was to cleanse himself immediately and thoroughly.

In ancient times, sanitary precautions were almost unheard of, but God gave His people some very strict guidelines about sanitation. Hands and feet were washed in preparation for almost any social event. One was to wash before eating. If people touched a dead body, they were to wash themselves in running water and allow time for drying in the sun. They were also to change into other clothes that had been washed and dried beforehand. After an outbreak of staph infections in several New England hospitals, the New York State Department of Health issued some new instructions about hospital personnel washing their hands. Their instructions were almost identical to those given in the Bible in Numbers 19.

There are places in the world today where human waste is just dumped out in the streets where people walk. That was the way it was disposed of in most places in the world up until just a hundred years ago. But 3,500 years ago, God told His people, "Go outside the camp, dig a hole and bury it." The pagan nations that were suffering from cholera, dysentery, and typhoid fever must have wondered how the Hebrews managed to stay so healthy. The reason was they were obeying God's health rules and sanitation laws.

God told the ancient Hebrews to separate people who had infectious diseases from the healthy. We would call that **quarantine**. God's Word said they were to avoid becoming intoxicated, and although alcohol was the only drug known in that age, God's health instructions included (by implication) the recreational use of other kinds of drugs.

Males were to be circumcised, God said. Why? Circumcision was a physical sign that identified a man as a member of God's Covenant People. It was also a health precaution. It was not until the 1940s that medical science documented the way circumcision prevents infections in both males and females (including cervical cancer in women), but God knew 3,500 years ago that was a good idea.

God also instructed His people to be moral in their behavior. Does morality affect a person's health? It certainly does. Psychologist Henry C. Link says there is a definite connection between sin and some diseases, and psychiatrist William Sadler claims a guilty conscience can produce some emotional disorders.

God said His people should not engage in premarital or extra-marital sex, homosexuality, or prostitution. The outbreaks of syphilis, gonorrhea, and other sexually transmitted diseases have crippled populations for centuries, but not the ancient Hebrews or anyone else who was living according to God's prescription for good health.

CHANGE IN LIFE STYLE REQUIRED

God's instructions to the Hebrews through Moses required them by faith to accept some ideas and practices that were different from what most people accepted, and contrary to the advice of the best secular experts of that day. God was insisting that the Hebrews change their lifestyle in some peculiar and inconvenient ways.

It is not easy to change familiar ways of doing things even when the familiar ways are disastrous. For example, in the Vienna Medical Center in the mid 1800s, one out of every six women who entered the obstetrical ward died, and more than half the surgical patients died. Dr. Ignaz Semmelweis was in charge of one obstetrical unit. He observed that physicians began their day by doing autopsies on bodies of people who had died the night before. Then, without washing their hands, they proceeded to do pelvic exams and deliveries with living patients. Semmelweis concluded they must be transporting something infectious from dead bodies to living ones.

Dr. Semmelweis instituted new rules in his unit — the same Old Testament rules about washing and changing clothes. The mortality rate in his ward dropped in three months from one in six to one in 84. It was an astonishing achievement.

Was Semmelweis praised or promoted for his life-saving discovery? No. His new rules were considered so radical that they were rejected and he was fired. It took many more years, more dead patients, and work of more influential people (Louis Pasteur, Sir Joseph Lister) to prove Semmelweis' discovery.

SIMILAR PROBLEM WITH AIDS

There are a lot of diseases today that result from poor choices in lifestyle. The one that currently gets most of the nation's attention is AIDS. It is that old reluctance to change from an unhealthy lifestyle to a healthy lifestyle that makes AIDS such a threat.

We are being told continually that what is needed to combat AIDS is more education about it. But the so-called "AIDS education" that is suggested by the people leading the parade has a social focus rather than a health focus. The primary purpose of what is called "AIDS education" seems to be to legitimize sexual perversion and immorality. The secondary purpose is to generate more dollars to search for a medicine that can replace morality as the sure cure.

Consider what we know about AIDS: It is said to have begun primarily in the homosexual community and for a time was limited to people who engaged in homosexuality. In the last few years, it has spread through IV drug use and bisexual immorality and prostitution into the heterosexual population.

Recent statistics from the federal Centers for Disease Control (USA Today, 4/93) indicate 64% of men who have

AIDS contracted it from homosexual contacts, 20% got it through IV drug use, and 16% were infected through prostitutes, bisexual or heterosexual activity, blood transfusions, etc. Of the women who currently have AIDS, 50% became infected through IV drug use, 36% through prostitution or bisexual activity, 7% by blood transfusion, 7% through other sources.

Now ask yourself, "What would happen if Americans began living as we once did by this Divine Design for Good Health?" About 84% of the AIDS problems would be solved quickly, and within a short while there would be no more contaminated blood infecting people receiving transfusions.

During President Clinton's "World AIDS Day" speech at Georgetown Medical Center, a heckler interrupted and accused the President of "doing nothing" about AIDS. Of course that is not the case. The federal government is spending about $1.8 billion annually on AIDS research and service programs (more than it spends on any other disease). AIDS is one of the easiest diseases to prevent, but the fact is that neither the President nor Congress nor any government agency can make the moral or lifestyle decisions for the heckler, or for you and me.

The Bible says, "When you live the healthy lifestyle God tells you to live, you are not likely to have that kind of disease."

Do I believe in divine healing? Yes, I believe God can do miracles. He can, has, and will continue to miraculously heal people's illnesses when He determines that needs to be done.

Does God answer "Yes" to every prayer for divine healing? Obviously not. If He did so, who would ever die? Do we not always pray for the healing for sick people whom we care about? The human body is programmed to become ill and to eventually die. The best way to protect one's health and extend one's life is not to violate every rule of healthy behavior and then pray for miraculous healing, but to live consistently by the Divine Design for Good Health.

MAINTAINING MENTAL AND EMOTIONAL HEALTH

Any discussion of health must also include mental and emotional health. The Bible speaks to that. Philippians 4:7 tells us that if we follow the Divine Design for Good Health, "The peace of God, which passeth all understanding, shall keep your hearts and minds through Christ Jesus."

Physicians estimate that 60% or more of their patients who come to them for treatment of physical ailments are really suffering from mental or emotional problems. The mind can produce symptoms of illness in the body. Turmoil at the emotional center of your life does three things physically:

1. It changes the amount of blood flowing to some of your physical organs.
2. It affects the secretions of certain glands (adrenal glands, for example).
3. It changes the amount of tension in the muscles of the body. (It may also lower your resistance to infections.)

When one's body is subjected over a period of time to repeated assaults by negative mental and emotional signals, the result can be pain, high blood pressure, kidney disease, heart disease, gastrointestinal disorders, or hardening of the arteries. Even before the physical damage has been done, mental and emotional problems can make one's life miserable.

One of the most common mental and emotional problems is mental stress. Every person has to deal with situations that produce stress, but not everyone reacts to stress the same way.

Three things help relieve stress:

1. Balance stressful experiences with stress-relieving activities.
2. Break up periods of stress with periods of rest.
3. Develop a positive and peaceful attitude.

People who react to stress by what the Bible calls "carnal thinking" suffer real damage in mind and body. Carnal thinking (Galatians 5:19) includes such things as immoral thinking, hatred and fighting, jealousy and anger, selfishness, complaining and criticizing, resentment and envy. If that is the way you typically think or react you are damaging yourself more than anyone else.

If you visit Yellowstone National Park and watch the grizzly bears in the area, you will learn that the grizzly is the most ferocious animal in North America and considers itself king of the wilderness. Grizzly bears will drive away all animals that compete with it for food. But there is one animal that the grizzly will tolerate — that is the skunk. Why will the grizzly let a skunk eat beside him? Could he not kill a skunk as easily as he might kill other rivals? Yes! But the grizzly is smart enough to know that the result of attacking a skunk is so unpleasant, he is better off leaving the skunk alone.

The Bible reminds us that the carnal way of thinking is so self-destructive, we are better off leaving it alone. Jesus said it this way: "Love your enemies; bless them that curse you; do good to them that hate you, and pray for them who despitefully use you, and persecute you."

Colossians 3:5–9 tells us to get rid of immorality, perversion, covetousness, anger, malice, and dishonesty, and also to get hold of mercy, kindness, humility, patience, forgivenes,s and love. How do we do that? The best way is to give ourselves to the

Lord, for when His Holy Spirit is filling our lives it produces in us "Love, joy, peace, patience, gentleness, goodness, faith, responsiveness to God and temperance" (Galations 5:22,23).

In his book <u>Practice of Psychiatry</u>, Dr. William Sadler wrote that an "amazingly large percentage of human disease and suffering is directly traceable ... to unwholesome thinking and unclean living." He claimed that "the sincere acceptance of the principles and teachings of Christ with respect to peace and joy, unselfishness and clean living would at once wipe out more than half of the difficulties, diseases, and sorrows of the human race" (pp. 64–65).

The Lord gives us His divine directions for good health so we will not have to endure the all too common miseries of the human spirit.

RECEIVING SPIRITUAL HEALTH

Our verse in John's third letter speaks about the "prosperity" or "well-being" of the soul as well as the body. Those two are certainly related, and any questions for good health are not complete until one has discovered how he can receive spiritual health.

The Bible says every person who does not know or belong to the Lord is "spiritually dead" (Ephesians 2:2–5 and 5:14; Colossians 2:13). That term "spiritually dead" makes it clear the unsaved person is not well spiritually. One does not decide to become "spiritually dead" for that is the natural condition of unregenerate humans. The fundamental decision we all face is whether or not we want to become "spiritually alive" (or "well in the soul").

Generally speaking, physical health is something we receive through our parents when we are in our mother's womb, and after our birth, we choose by our behavior whether or not we will maintain the health that has been given to us. Mental and emotional health generally come out of our environment and personal choices about our attitudes and reactions. We or our parents contribute a lot to those two areas. Spiritual health is different in that neither we nor our families can supply it. It can be received only as a "gift from God" (Romans 6:23). For centuries it has been known that within every person, there is a basic conflict raging between two opposing forces. Sigmund Freud thought it was a struggle with the sexual impulses. Alfred Adler saw it as a conflict between one's selfish instincts and social instincts. Dr. Karl Menninger called it a contest between the life instinct and the death instinct. He said it is as though a person is standing at the top of a tall cliff and hears one voice saying "Jump! Jump!" and another voice saying, "Turn around and come to safety."

The Bible gets to the essence of it, explaining that every person has to deal with the downward, destructive drawing of Satan and also has to deal with the upward call of God. In the book of Romans, the Apostle Paul describes his own inner conflict between these two opposing attractions. This internal battle is the most important battle a person faces in life, for the outcome determines one's nature and character and conduct and destiny.

You don't have to be a genius to understand that you need to resist Satan's downward drag and respond to God and His upward call. Dr. Carl Jung said the most common problem he found in his patients 35 years and older was the need for religious faith.

But how do we shun Satan and get to God? The Apostle Paul explained that he did that by receiving the saving grace of Jesus Christ. "I thank God there is a way out in Jesus Christ ... for the law of the Spirit of life in Christ Jesus hath made me free from the law of sin and death. For what human effort could not do, God did by sending His Son to die for our sin" (Romans 7:25 and 8:2–3).

If you want to maximize potential for good health in body, mind, and emotions you must accept the Divine Design for Good Health. If you want to be well in your soul, you must decide you are going to turn away from Satan and the way of sin and turn in faith to the Lord Jesus, claiming His gift of saving grace.

PASSWORD

Text: Matthew 21:22   Kenneth Twigg Whalum

And all things, whatsoever ye shall ask in prayer believing, ye shall receive.   (Matthew 21:22)

Having March 23, 1934, for a birthday has qualified me for all the diseases of old age. I have parts of this old machine breaking down that I had not even realized existed earlier. Strange how difficult it is to describe pain in unfamiliar places.

Prostate disorders are commonplace with old men (I don't know about other animals), so I have been told not to be surprised at the process of deterioration. People have a way of explaining away others' infirmities as if nothing is a real problem. Many of us would be better off without advice of fellow sufferers along the path to old age.

My urologist was busy until late afternoon on the day I went to see him; impertinence, lack of patience, and God's will combined to send me on a search for a doctor who could see me sooner, because I had promised myself that as soon as I had finished a very rigorous political campaign, the next morning would find me in the doctor's office to seek relief from the pains

I had suffered throughout the season of rallies, forums, street-corner advertising, and endorsement interviews.

The second doctor could see me that morning, as his aide informed me when I dashed in his office without an appointment. Doctors' offices, in spite of telling intentions, are not comfortable places for patients. When finally you are ushered into a treatment room, pricked with needles, subjected to the squeeze of rubber straps to enlarge veins, partially disrobed, and nervously anxious, the wait has just begun. But you are there for the duration and nothing will make a minute pass in fewer than 60 seconds.

This young, newlywed doctor entered with the usual greetings. (I always remind myself that doctors practice medicine, an art in which they never become perfect, as is witnessed by the fact that we always have to tell them what we think is wrong and where we hurt before they can even begin to put their knowledge to practice — they are always practicing, which I use here in the same sense as those who rehearse.) The major difference with this young medic, however, is that after a few words, he laid hands on me and prayed one of the most comforting prayers I have ever heard. In his prayer he acknowledged his frailty before God and pleaded for the help, power, and wisdom of an all-knowing, all-seeing, all-wise God. Trust me when I say I have never felt so comfortable in a treatment room in all the days of my life.

We have, most of us, a lot of confidence in doctors about whose backgrounds we know precious little and whose credentials we never check. I can think of no better recommendation to those who are sick than to suggest they see a doctor who recognizes the limits of his/her abilities and has the wisdom to seek help from the Healer.

The passage of scripture in which this message has its base records a very busy time in the life of our Savior and Lord. He is beginning to prepare people for His ultimate departure from among them. He is on a cleanup mission, and He is passionate about His teaching and His actions. You have to know God really well to have a triumphal march into Death Row. He does not seem to be even concerned about the outcome as it relates to Himself, but is deeply immersed in His feelings for His people. The inference is that when He entered Jerusalem, He commanded so much attention that the people of the city wanted to know what kind of person has created the furor attendant to this stranger. And the trailing multitude informed them, "Hast thou not known, hast thou not even heard? This is Jesus, the Prophet of Nazareth of Galilee."

He clarifies church purpose and quickly shows to whom church resources belong when He exerts unusual strength and fortitude by casting out the money changers and overturning their sales counters, making a myth of skeptics' belief that Jesus was a mild-mannered, weak, and timid character. Exiting Jerusalem, He enters Bethany and demonstrates how useless anything is that does not serve its intended purpose only to end with a strong lesson on the value of faith.

To the subject: There is no pathway that leads from **asking** to **receiving** that bypasses **believing**. **Password** is described as a secret word that allows a person speaking it to pass a guard and enter into an otherwise closed door. Those who **ask** seek to **receive,** but there is a locked door between the two which can only be opened by the password — **believe.**

The major ingredient in the process of healing is, therefore, faith. It ought be our greatest desire in life to please God, and yet we know that without faith it is **impossible** to please Him. Pleasing God and the desire to be healed cannot be mutually exclusive; rather they make a dynamic duo. **Knowing** that God can heal is prerequisite to believing that He will. The Hebrews make clear that if there is any doubt concerning what God will do it can be countered by what God can do. Their strong point in opposing the king's demands was that their God is **able.**

Very simply put, if you will take a malfunctioning Chevrolet back to General Motors to be fixed strictly on the fact that they made it, or a disabled GE washing machine back to General Electric for the same reason, taking a malfunctioning body part to the author and finisher is not such a bad idea. The kind of trust we vest in manufacturers would be a good beginning for a new relationship with God the Creator — "it is God who hath made us and not we ourselves" (Psalms 100). Things and people do break down, and it is good to keep the warranty updated. Shade-tree mechanics are not recommended where good repair jobs are needed. It is far superior to "return to sender," for warranties are not effective except at the place of origin. Ford warranties are not acceptable at Chrysler dealerships.

Satan is a great door-locker, and faithlessness tightens the jamb. It is not Satan's desire that we exercise healing faith; he would much rather we be sick and helpless and hopeless. He often uses our sickness to weaken our faith and cast doubt on God's ability to heal. He stresses for us the numbers, for instance, who die of cancer and never shines a light on those who have confounded doctors by surviving. Isn't it interesting how soon we give up on God and how easy it is for the devil to command our attention. Stop right now, and see if you can't remember a cancer survivor, a stroke survivor, a pneumonia survivor, a tuberculosis survivor. There are countless testimonies where, during preparatory to surgery, the x-rays showed the blockage or the tumor was gone. Satan would have us believe the cases were misdiagnosed, and yet in your heart of hearts you know God granted healing. Even an old World War II song advises us to "accentuate the positive, eliminate the negative." Better to magnify one case of healing than to rehearse 1,000 deaths from sickness.

Colon cancer is prevalent in America, and many live in morbid fear of contracting this malady. Circumstances have sent me on two trips to the operating table for colon surgery, separated by 23 years; the fact that they were round trips and that I am preaching this sermon a year after the second forms a valid basis upon which I can proclaim victory in Jesus and that God heals.

And there is no cancer in my body!

We board city and interstate buses without checking drivers' credentials. We board planes without even being concerned about pilots' names. We open canned goods and eat the contents without concern for poisons or contaminants. We trust opposing traffic to stay on its side of the yellow line on streets and highways as we exceed speed limits. We trust restaurants not to serve us spoiled food without knowing the cooks. We trust elevators for safe descent. We trust eyedrops to be irritant-free. We trust pharmacists to correctly fill our prescriptions.

But we experience serious difficulty trusting in the God of Abraham, Isaac, and Jacob, in spite of the fact He alone has brought us. The devil has taught us to blame God when bad comes and to claim luck when things break our way. Moses was not without purpose when he constantly reminded the Israelites through the Pentateuch that it was God who had brought them. How soon we forget. The question has been asked, "Is there anything too hard for God?"

There is a story recorded in the Lord's Gospel of Luke 13:11, concerning a woman who had suffered the same illness for 18 years. She was bowed together, that is to say she was bent completely over so that her head was between her legs. Please imagine how miserable it must have been to spend 6,574 days in pain and discomfort looking between your legs at where you were coming from and never able to see where you're going. The inference is that she had tried many times to lift herself up to no avail. Imagine the pain of a curved spine without any manner of a painkiller. Even if she tried to sit down, her legs would be pointed up to the sky and her back would never get any relief.

Then one day while Jesus was teaching in the synagogue on the Sabbath, this woman caught His attention, and with characteristic compassion He loosed her from her infirmity and laid His hands on her, straightening her up immediately.

The religious leaders in the synagogue were angered because He had healed her on the Sabbath. Imagine 18 years of suffering, one day of healing, and the people were angry. The scriptures do not say she had come to the synagogue for healing and perhaps she had not, but the fact is she was healed at "church" because she had dared to come near where Jesus was.

Satan will always seek to hinder your healing and will even try to convince you of all the reasons you should not be healed and why Jesus will not heal you. He was not even willing to let this woman rejoice in her healing, but rather sought to catch her up in a "religious" technicality. We gain so much just for being where Jesus is. Wherever God has placed a period, don't you dare replace it with a comma. Don't let a closed door come between you and Jesus — He is the **Healer**. Use the password to draw ever closer to Him. **Believe and receive**. Two songs come to mind as I close this:

We are our Heavenly Father's Children
And we all know that He loves us, one and all.
Yet, there are times when we find we answer
Another voice's call.
But if we are willing He will teach us
His voice only to obey no matter where.
And He knows, yes He knows
Just how much we can bear.

Think of the times you've asked the question
Down in your heart, "Lord, just what shall I do?"
Then you confide in your friends and loved ones,
But they have troubles, too.
There is a God who rules Earth and Heaven,
In Him there's relief for every pain or care.
And He knows, yes He knows,
Just how much we can bear.

Though the load gets heavy
You're never left alone to bear it all.

Just ask for strength and keep on toiling
Though the teardrops fall.
You have the joy of this assurance,
The Heavenly Father will always answer prayer.
And He knows, yes He knows,
Just how much
We can bear.

You can make it.
You can make it.
That problem you're going through.
God's gonna show you what to do.
You can make it.
You can make it.
The problem that's got you down.
God's gonna turn it all around.
You can make it.
You can make it.
I don't care what's going wrong.
God won't let it last too long.
You're not in this thing alone.
You can make it.

Believing is the bridge to **receiving**. **Belief** equals **receipt**.
Password! Password! Password! Pray this prayer every time
you doubt:

God, grant me the faith to trust and never doubt.
Grant me the grace to wait on you. Grant me the
courage to endure, the mercy to sustain, and the love
to feel your presence. **AMEN**.

SILENCE AT THE TURNING POINTS

Text: Job 2:11–13   Nancy Hastings Sehested

*Y*ears ago I was visiting a man, Mr. Watkins, in the hospital. He was very seriously ill, so they were keeping him in the Intensive Care Unit (ICU). I was visiting the man daily. There was a possibility that he would die at any time.

In the waiting room was his wife, Mrs. Watkins, keeping vigil on a plastic-coated couch. Mrs. Watkins had to wait for two-hour intervals to see her husband. As clergy, I could walk in anytime. Mrs. Watkins walked me from the waiting room down the long corridor to the ICU double doors. As we walked, I asked her how she was doing.

Suddenly, without any warning, Mrs. Watkins shoved me up against the wall and screamed for all to hear, "I know why you are here. You are here to steal my husband away from me. I'm here to tell you that I won't let that happen."

Mrs. Watkins was good on her word. She didn't let that happen, and neither did I.

I scooted away quickly, rubbing my shoulder and puzzling over how Mrs. Watkins could have ever gotten the idea that I was out to nab her dying husband.

It was right there at the double doors to ICU that I experienced some new revelations. Clergy work is a lot more physically dangerous than I had ever imagined. People who are suffering can exhibit some uncharacteristically violent behavior. Asking distraught people how they are is dangerous, and one should proceed with caution. Experience can be a swift and direct teacher.

When I reached Mr. Watkins, he was weak, but alert. I read some Bible passages to him. I lifted up a prayer for him. And then, just before I left as I held his hand, I asked him, "Mr. Watkins, is there anything I can tell your wife for you?"

He turned his head and looked away from me at the wall for a minute. Over 60 years they had been together. These two had become one. Was he looking at a wall that now was about to separate them from the only life they'd known, a wall of death? Mr. Watkins turned back to me. He said nothing. I repeated the question, "Mr. Watkins, is there anything I can tell your wife for you?"

Now his eyes filled with tears. There were no words. His tears did the talking for him. Words were too meager an offering. There was only silence at this jolting turning point.

Today's sermon is not for everyone. Actually, it is rare to have a sermon that touches everyone. But, today, especially, I am aware that perhaps these words are only for a few. The rest of you can store them away for future use. If you just won the Publisher's Clearinghouse Sweepstakes, this sermon is not for you. If you just received a salary raise, this sermon is not for you. If you just had a complete physical check-up and you are in terrific condition, then this sermon is not for you.

This sermon is for those of you who have known the silence of the turning points. It is for those of you who are ready to ask some questions. "Why am I suffering?" "How can I talk about God in the face of so much suffering?" It is for Malinda and Gale fighting for their lives with cancer. It is for Amy in grief. It is for Ben with AIDS. It is for those who say, "This is too much." It is for all of you who are feeling that we as a nation have never been in so much confusion, chaos, and suffering.

What? Do you need reminding of the troubles of our times? Every hour $33.7 million is spent on the perceived dangers outside our country. We have yet to realize that the greatest threats are dangers within our country. We have moved far, far away from making human beings our priority … especially vulnerable human beings like our children, our sick, our elderly. Every hour $8.7 million is spent on the savings and loan bailout. Every hour $23.6 million is spent on the national debt. The Chair of Coca-Cola makes $41,346 an hour.

We are double-locking our doors. Fanaticism is on the rise. Fear seems the one characteristic that we hand out to everyone, equally. Some people are calling our times the "shipwreck" time, when every part of our society is falling apart.

What is the church to do? Do we yell at our tumbling structures to change? Do we create new structures to pick up the pieces? What do we do? The troubles of Job are upon us. Where is there healing?

Job knew trouble. Double trouble. Job had believed the theology of blessing. His faith had taught him that if he was good and righteous then God would bless him with goodness. His life was a picture of perfection. He had a family, wealth, health, and happiness. He had fulfilled the American dream, the self-made man of fortune. Only good things happened to this very good man. Job gave God all the praise. He counted his many blessings, named them one by one, and thanked God Almighty. The Bible says that Job was "blameless and upright, one who feared God, and turned away from evil" (Job 1:1). Job was "the richest man in the east" (Job 1:3). God was in the heavens, and all was right with the world.

Then the Adversary (called "Satan" in the Revised Standard Version) stepped into the heavens and made a wager with God. The Adversary bet that if God took away everything that Job had, then Job would curse God.

Tragedy struck suddenly with one tidal wave of disaster after another. The Sabeans attacked the oxen and servants. Lightning struck and burned up the sheep and servants. The Chaldeans raided and killed the camels and the servants. A hurricane wind pulled the roof off the house and killed his children. Job rent his clothes amid the ruins and still held to his faith. "The Lord gave, and the Lord has taken away; blessed be the name of the Lord" (Job 1:21).

The last affliction came to Job's own body. Sores came upon him, covering him from head to toe. Job's three friends heard of the horrors that had come upon him. When they first came for their pastoral visit, they could see that Job was suffering unbearably. They offered the best of good friendship. For seven days they sat with Job in the deep silence that comes from unimaginable suffering. They offered their compassion with their presence. We should never underestimate the healing power of presence in the midst of suffering and pain.

After their week of silence, the friends opened their mouths and blew it. They asked Job what terrible sins he had committed to deserve this trouble. By this time, Job was distraught. Job cursed the day he was born. Job had good cause to sing the spiritual, "Oh, Nobody Knows the Trouble I've Seen."

And what about you? Does anyone know the troubles you've seen? Does anyone know the troubles we've seen together as a nation?

Buried in an avalanche of troubles, Job spoke to God. Job cried out to God, "I will speak in the anguish of my spirit; I will complain in the bitterness of my soul" (Job 7:11). Job cries the ancient cry of the ages in the face of suffering, "Why me, Lord?" And God is silent. "I cry to you, and you do not answer me; I stand, and you do not heed me," Job prayed (Job 30:20).

When Rabbi Yohanan, son of Zakkai, lost his son, his disciples tried to console him. Rabbi Eliezer reminded him that the same tragedy had struck Adam, who knew how to overcome his grief. But Rabbi Yohanan, son of Zakkai, replied: "Is my own grief not enough? Must you add Adam's?"

Then Rabbi Yehoshus reminded him of the ordeals endured by Job, who allowed himself to be consoled. But Rabbi Yohanan, son of Zakkai, replied: "Is my own sorrow not enough? Why do you wish to add that of Job?"

Then Rabbi Yassi reminded him of Aaron the high priest, who witnessed the death of his two sons and knew how to contain his grief and remain silent. And Rabbi Yohanan, son of Zakkai, replied: "Is my own anguish not deep enough? Must you add that of Aaron?" (Told by Elie Wiesel in Messengers of God)

Everyone suffers alone. Yet, no suffering is limited to oneself. To be human is to know suffering. Yet that is little consolation in the midst of heartache. To say, "I suffer," and then be reminded, "Well, we all suffer," does not bring an end to my suffering.

Still the question bobs to the top, "Why?" How does one speak of God after tremendous tragedy? How does one speak of God after something as massive in human tragedy as the Holocaust?

A friend of mine is a religion teacher in college. When the class studied theodicy, they took a look at two writers' responses to the Holocaust. Richard Rubenstein says that after the Holocaust, it is time to give up on God. He writes that after the Holocaust, there were no categories that remained to talk about God.

On the other hand, Holocaust survivor Elie Wiesel took a different perspective. He says that there is never any way to justify suffering. If you think God punishes to teach you something, what could you teach 6 1/2 million Jews who were killed? Wiesel says the only response is to make a protest to God, lodge a complaint. But don't give up on God. He says that if we say, "There is no God, " then the Nazis have won.

For the college students, they named the suffering of the

world, and Job's name came up. These college students decided after reading Job that suffering is to teach you something or it is to punish you for something. Their answers were no better than Job's three friends who tried to explain suffering in just the same way.

The story of Job is not about patient suffering. Job is terribly impatient. Other sermons would have to explore what the book does and does not say. But it does ask the question about God — how do we speak of God in the suffering? Does God care? Where is God?

Charlene and her husband, Milton, had been married for 13 years. They wanted a child so much. They tried so hard to have one on their own. Charlene had six miscarriages in the first 10 years of their marriage. They gave up that direction and headed into another. They adopted a baby girl.

At Charlene and Milton's house, heaven had come on earth. They could not have been happier or prouder. Charlene went overboard on buying dresses for the baby. Milton went overboard on taking pictures of the baby. Life was good. God had answered their prayers.

Then one night there was a fire in their home. They couldn't get to their daughter's room in time. She died. Twenty months old, and she died. Milton suffered injuries and was hospitalized. Charlene escaped physical harm.

I went to visit Charlene. Charlene did not greet me. She said no word. I sat beside her, opened a Psalm, and read it. Charlene said nothing. Silence. Words did not come to me anymore. We sat in silence, side by side. I couldn't tell you how long we sat that way. One hour? Two? Who knows. The silence of suffering knows no time.

A Baptist clergywoman shared with me her story one night when we sat up late after her ordination service. Peggy had three daughters. Ten years before, her middle daughter was killed in a car accident late one night. She was 16 years old. I asked her what it was that helped her to live through such a tragedy. Peggy said: "I died that night. I died. Once you've died in this life, you have nothing left to lose. You don't have to be afraid again. You can go on living."

I asked, "How did you get through those first weeks of shock?" She explained:

I was immobilized. I could not get out of bed. I could not get dressed. I could not speak at all. I was silent. Three of my friends came over without asking. They moved in with me. They cooked meals I did not want to eat. They dressed me in clothes that I did not want to wear. The first week, they sat with me in silence. Church people tried to say the right word, the comforting word. There were none for me. There was only silence. Silence. That is the language that speaks in the turning points of tragedy. God was in the silence and suffering with me.

Hasn't the world hit such a turning point of tragedy that we are in the shock of silence? Isn't it time for God's church to sit with the world's suffering, offer our comfort and presence in silence, and wait for God? Where is God? Can God speak to us in this silence? Perhaps it is in the silence that the healing begins.

We are silent. We sit. We wait. And there is a man of sorrows acquainted with grief who sits with us in this silence. The everlasting arms of God are holding us and catching our tears. The healing presence of the Holy One is here, in this turning point of silence.

HEAVEN'S HEALTH CARE PLAN

James M. Latimer

*T*o a great extent, the evangelical church has been hood-winked on the subject of healing. Dr. Benjamin Breckenridge Warfield, a Princeton Seminary professor of many years ago, proposed a theological position that has become known as Cessationist Theology. This basic position is that after the last Apostle died and the 12 original Apostles had finished their work and ministry, the miracle gifts, those gifts that would include healing, ceased to exist and were no longer a part of our world. His position was that they were there only for the time that it would take for the scriptures that we know today as the New Testament to be canonized, and after that there would be no need for the miracle gifts. Dr. Warfield was a well-respected theologian of the Reform Tradition. I have read a great deal of his works, and I have utilized his position, on occasion, because he was honored throughout the Kingdom. Thus, to a large degree, and for many years, the evangelical church has failed to enjoy and participate in the reality of the broadness of the working of the Holy Spirit because they have been taught that the Holy Spirit would lead people to Christ, and that He could do a few things, but He was not involved in the miraculous sign gifts as He was in the Apostolic Age. However, there are many today, including myself, who have re-thought that position. I believe that God does heal today. I don't believe that God heals everybody in every particular instance in their life because, if He did, nobody would ever die. That is contrary to the Bible because it states specifically that it is appointed unto man once to die, and after that, the judg-ment. So death is a part of God's plan for life for eternity. Death is the natural end of life, but that does not preclude God from healing. God is not limited, and He has not put Himself into a position where He cannot heal.

Health care is not only something of a political football with some people wanting this and some people wanting that, but it has also become a very personal issue in our lives due to the pain and suffering that we experience in our own maladies, as well as in others'. I had a lady stop me today, as I was working on this.

She asked me to pray for her and told me that her arthritis was getting unbearable. Now that is a reality. It is a health care problem. And, when it is your own fingers, arms, or legs that ache, you understand the problem of health care, and it is not just something of political debate or a socio-economic situation. It is a personal situation in which all of us are involved. We have raised our children and know about coughs, wheezes, and sneezes and all those kinds of things. Health is a very active sit-uation that we deal with in our lives on a daily basis. Additionally, a major portion of the health care debate is the high cost of health care and the details that are involved in get-ting treatment for health care. Sometimes we feel absolutely helpless to do anything when people are suffering. The finan-cial drain and the emotional drain are sometimes as great as the physical drain.

For the believer, health care is more than a socio-political debate. It has, and is, a spiritual dimension. In Exodus 15:26, God says, "For I am the Lord who heals you." The word for healing is "rapha." We have the words Jehovah Rapha, the God who heals you, and Yahweh, your Physician. There are countless incidents documented in scripture of how God has healed. Sometimes God heals directly. Sometimes we see God work through the manifestations of the Prophets, through His Son the Lord Jesus, through the Apostles, and through others who had the gift of healing.

As the subject of divine healing is discussed, several questions come to light. Individuals ask: "What about medicine?" "Is it all right to go to a doctor?" "Should you ever go to a doctor at all, or should you just pray for everything that is wrong with you?" "Why are some people not healed, and why does it seem that the people we want healed don't get healed, and the people that God chooses to heal are the people we would let suffer?" There are times we don't see any sense in the way God heals. Then the question: "What about faith healers, people who go on television with the bright lights on them and have thousands of people lined up who have testimonies of being healed?" Then you hear later that there were microphones and earphones and that some of that really wasn't true. "What is the difference between a healing and a miracle?" "Does God really heal today?"

The only place to go for answers such as these is to God's Word. In II Kings 20:1–11, we have the story of Hezekiah's illness. In verse one, it reads, "In those days, Hezekiah was sick and near death, and Isaiah the Prophet, the son of Amos, went to him and said to him, 'Thus saith the Lord, Set your house in order for you shall die and not live.'" Can you imagine being faced with that today? For your pastor to come to you and to say, "All right, Brother, Sister, set your house in order. Your days are limited, and you are going to die." There would be all kinds of pandemonium going on, and that is exactly what happened. Isaiah walked into King Hezekiah's sick room. Hezekiah is sick unto death, and the preacher comes in and says, "You need to straighten your house because you are going to die." Well, that is not a very comforting message. When I was in seminary, they told us to be a little bit cooler than that when you go in. Even if you know they are going to die, don't be so blunt about it. However, Isaiah used the direct approach and confronted Hezekiah with God's statement. Then Hezekiah turned his face toward the wall, and he prayed to the Lord saying, "Lord, remember me, I pray, how I walked before You in truth and with a loyal heart and have done what is good in Your sight."

And, Hezekiah wept bitterly. Here is a case of a man who was sick unto death and told from the Prophet of God that he was going to die, and yet he turned around and poured his heart out to God. Then the fourth verse says,

> And it happened before Isaiah had gone out into the middle court, the word of the Lord came to him, "Return and tell Hezekiah, the leader of My people, 'Thus says the Lord God of David your father, I have heard your prayer, I have seen your tears; surely I will heal you. On the third day you shall go up to the house of the Lord.'"

In other words, instead of being dead, in three days, God said he would be totally well and be worshipping in the house of God. And, he says in verse six, "'I will add to your days 15 years, and I will deliver you and this city from the hand of the king of Assyria; and I will defend the city for My own sake and the sake of My servant David.' And Isaiah said, 'Take a lump of figs." And they took and laid it on the boil, and he recovered. Now we have a situation where God has said the man was going to die. The man turned to God and asked for healing, and God has responded and told him that he will live, but, even then, uses the medicine of the day for treatment. Hezekiah then complicates things by asking Isaiah, "What is the sign that the Lord will heal me, that I should go up to the house of the Lord on the third day?" Even though God has told him that He is going to heal him, Hezekiah wants an affirmation. Isaiah replied, "This shall be a sign to you from the Lord, that the Lord will do the thing which He has spoken: shall the shadow go forward 10 degrees or backwards 10 degrees?" Hezekiah answered, "It is an easy thing for the shadow to go down 10 degrees; no, let the shadow go backwards 10 degrees." Now there was a staircase in the palace that one of the earlier kings had built. The way it was built, it could be used as a sundial. What Hezekiah was saying was that he wanted a sign, and that he wanted the sign to be that this sundial would move. The movement of the sun around the sundial is very slow and not easy to discern, much like watching paint dry. Hezekiah said that he wanted the sundial to move 10 degrees, and not only move 10 degrees, but to move 10 degrees backwards. And, indeed, that is exactly what happened.

I am sure that several, if not all, of the questions we asked earlier came to the mind of Isaiah as he was dealing with Hezekiah's healing. Here God has made a statement through His Prophet that Hezekiah is going to die. Yet, because of Hezekiah's prayer and his faith, God relents and sends Isaiah back to express this change of mind. Isaiah prescribes a medical poultice current to that day that obviously God wanted to be used in the healing process.

God even presented another sign for Hezekiah to give him an affirmation of the healing. Why did God first say that Hezekiah was going to die but then choose to heal him? Did God heal through the poultice or through a miracle? Did Isaiah also pray to heal Hezekiah? The only answer to these questions is that God is God and is beyond our limiting Him and putting Him into a box.

I think another aspect of our understanding healing versus miracles is to get a better grasp on what a miracle is. In the Book of Joshua we are told that the Jordan River stopped running for the Israelites to cross into the Promised Land.

There has been the theory that the clay banks that are found near Edom, somewhat above the point where the Israelites are thought to have crossed, caved in and prevented the flow of the Jordan's water. That very well may have been true. The fact that it happened at the particular time that God called for the Israelites to cross, and the fact that the Israelites still crossed on "dry land," and that the water started flowing again once the Israelites crossed, is a miracle. Even if God used natural processes of earthquakes, landslides, mighty winds, or whatever, for things to coincide in such a fashion as having already been prophesied is a miracle.

God never tells us in the Bible not to use medication. In fact, quite the contrary. He advocates such, as we have seen with Hezekiah. God has created all these things. He has given intelligence to those who apply the medical arts. And there are men and women of God whom God has raised up as purveyors of healing. In Colonial America, the preachers were the doctors. There were not any doctors in the community and very few educated people. The ministers were generally more highly educated than anyone else. They could read, and with the medical books from England, they primarily practiced medicine along with religion.

John Wesley, the great founder of the Methodist Church, wrote the first medical journal ever published in America. There needs to be that balance. And we need to understand that when we talk about faith healing, divine healing, and God's healing, we are not necessarily talking about anything that is exclusive of medicine. It could be exclusive, but it doesn't have to be. We need to avoid extremes on either side and not say that we haven't been healed unless God does it without medicine. Also, we don't need to be so pragmatic that we say we can only be healed through the medical process. God is the Creator, the Healer, the Consummator, and He can do what He wants to do.

The very basis of healing is compassion, and God's love is

full of compassion for us. When the Old Testament speaks of God's compassion, God's love, and God's comfort, the Hebrew word that is used is the word "racham." And that is the very same word that in another place is translated "womb." So, when God talks about His comfort, it is an all-encompassing love of protection and warmth, the very same as the human fetus finds in the womb.

There are four reasons why God heals. First of all, God heals in relation to our suffering. The healing ministry of Jesus was motivated by compassion and His deep personal concern for our suffering. In Matthew 14:13–14, it says, "When Jesus heard it, He departed from there by boat to a deserted place by Himself, but, when the multitude heard about it, they followed Him on foot from the cities. And when Jesus went out, He saw a great multitude, and He was moved with compassion for them, and He healed the sick."

There are other references as well. The lepers who came to Jesus, the Bible says Jesus had compassion on them. The demonized Jew, Jesus had compassion on him. Two blind men came in Matthew 20, and Jesus had compassion on them. Jesus also exemplified compassion in raising the widow's son when Jesus saw that it was her only son. In the feeding of the 4,000 in Matthew 15, Jesus performed one of His major miracles. He said, "These people have been here three days, and I have great compassion for them; give them something to eat." In Matthew 9:27, blind men who came to Jesus were healed because of the compassion of Christ. In Matthew 15, those who were demonized, Jesus had compassion on and healed. Also, in Luke 17, the healing of the lepers, and in Mark 5, the demon-possessed man, Jesus exhibited great compassion.

Compassion in its sheer volume of text should say to us that it is an all-important thing in the area of healing. As you read Matthew, Mark, Luke, and John, there is a consistency in statements of discovering that, as Jesus walked along, all He did was see people in great need, and He had compassion on them, lifted them up, healed them, and met whatever need they had. The heart of the matter boils down to understanding that the ministry of healing in the church is to establish ourselves not as a place where people can be healed, but as a place where people can find the love and compassion of the Lord.

God doesn't heal for excitement. Neither does He heal so that some of us can say that our theology is better than someone else's theology because God backed it up with healing. God doesn't use His compassion and healing to validate theology. God heals because God cares. If one really wants to be used by God and believes that God would work through him in a ministry of praying for those who are sick, one needs to be honest about the entire process and come to the point of understanding that there will be no glory for an individual at all.

The desire to want to work for God, to have a heart for God, and to have the compassion of God, has to be a prerequisite for a healing ministry. For a person desiring to be healed, it is important to remember that it is not who you are, what you have, or what you do, but that God wants to heal you because He loves you and has compassion for you. I have seen people desperately hurting, physically and emotionally, come with their head between their legs in shame because they didn't believe they have a right to be healed. Nobody has a right to be healed; nobody has earned the right to be healed. We are healed because God loves us and God has compassion for us and wants to touch us. If we believe in a compassionate favor, we ought to have the confidence to believe that He desires to heal the church today. For one to argue that Christ has withdrawn His healing ministry is tantamount to saying that Christ has withdrawn His compassion. That just does not jive with scripture.

Secondly, God heals in regard to His own Glory. In John 11, there is a marvelous story about Christ coming to the home of Martha and Mary after Lazarus died. In the fourth verse, Jesus and the disciples are around the Sea of Galilee, and word comes that Lazarus is sick. Jesus states, "This sickness is not unto death, but for the glory of God, that the Son of God may be glorified through it." After waiting awhile, Christ went there. Martha and Mary both came out and stated that, if Christ had been there earlier, Lazarus would not have died. Then we have that tremendous verse, "Jesus wept." I think this is one of the greatest verses in the Bible, again showing the great compassion of our Lord. But, then, when Christ did go to the grave and said for the stone to be taken away, His response to their reluctance was, "Did I not say to you that, if you would believe, you would see the glory of God?" And indeed Jesus did heal — Lazarus was raised from the dead.

In Jesus' ministry, He talked to the multitude, and they saw what Jesus was doing, and they marveled and glorified the God of Israel. In the third chapter of Acts, Peter, when confronted with a crippled man, stated, "Silver and gold have we none, but such as we have we give unto you: In the Name of Jesus, rise up and walk." The man then rose up and was jumping, shouting, and running all over the place and giving glory to God.

Throughout Luke's Gospel, the word that Luke uses for salvation is the very same word he uses for healing. He uses them interchangeably. As a physician, it was a major theme of Luke's Gospel. In the fifth chapter of Luke is the tremendous story of the friends who lowered the paralytic down through the roof, and it talks of how they glorified God in the healing. In Luke 7:12, there is in the City of Nain the widow's son who was healed and who glorified God. And, in Luke 1:13:11, there is the story of the woman bent double with all kinds of illnesses, and, when she was healed, she glorified God. The same was true in Luke 18:35 with the blind beggar on the Jericho Road. And, finally, in Luke 19:37, Luke speaks of the triumphant entry of Jesus into Jerusalem, and he said all the people glorified God because of the miracles and mighty works they had seen. Healing is for the glory of God, not for individuals' glory.

One of the problems today is that, if we are involved in praying for the sick, and someone is not healed, we think we look foolish if God doesn't heal. We have to bear in mind that healing is for the glory of God, not for our glory. The Bible tells us in I Corinthians 4:10, that we are to be "fools for Christ." We have got to be willing to be a fool for Christ's sake. John Wimber shares in his testimony that, years before he was saved, he saw a man in Los Angeles wearing a sign board. On the front of the sign board it said, "I am a fool for Christ." And on the back it asked the question, "Whose fool are you?" We all have to be somebody's fools. But, I would rather be a fool for Christ.

Jack Deere said that the Lord revealed to him years ago that, if he wouldn't take credit when someone was healed, then he would not have to worry about taking the blame when they were not healed. If you are sick and want to be healed, you begin by glorifying God, praising God, and praying for His compassion to bring healing.

The third reason that God heals today is in response to faith. God honors faith. I heard E. V. Hill preach on praise and Job. He said, "You know, Job just got stripped. I mean, boy, they just turned him every way but loose, took away everything he had, and the world caved in on top of him. Yet, he was still saying, 'Though I die, yet shall I praise Him.'" E. V. Hill said he could just imagine God running around heaven grabbing every angel He could lay a hand on and saying, "Come here! Look over here! Here's a man who has been stripped of everything, and all he wants to do is praise God." We need to be people who are like that, people who have the kind of faith that, regardless of what happens, have faith in God and believe in God all the way through.

In Matthew 9:20, there is the story of a woman who had been hemorrhaging for 12 years. The crowd had gathered around her, so she sneaked up behind Jesus to touch the hem of His garment. Her faith was so strong that Jesus turned around and said, "Who touched me?" Peter's response was, "What do you mean who touched you? There are 10,000 people out here jostling around. Everybody touched you." Jesus said, "No, you don't understand. Someone touched me with such great faith that I felt power go out of my body to heal." That is overwhelming faith that is honored by God.

It is also the story of the Canaanite woman whose daughter was demon-possessed. She had great faith in Jesus. In Matthew 9:2 is the story of those friends who had such faith that they lowered their friend through the roof. In Matthew 9:27–31, there is the story of the two blind men.

> When Jesus departed from there, the two blind men followed Him crying out, "Son of David, have mercy on us." When he had come into the house, the blind men came to Him, and Jesus said to them, "Do you believe that I am able to do this?" They said to Him, "Yes, Lord." And then He touched their eyes saying, "According to your faith, let it be done to you." And their eyes were opened, and Jesus sternly warned them saying, "Say to no one of this!" When they departed, they spread the news about Him in all that country.

These were two men who said they believed in Jesus and believed that Christ was able to heal. If we come to Jesus with a malady or problem in our life, I believe the first question we need to ask ourselves about faith is, "Do I hear Jesus asking, 'Do you believe that I am able to do this?'" I don't care what that illness is. I don't care what the need is in your heart. You need to hear the Lord Jesus say to you, "Do you believe that I am able to do this?" You need to have the faith to answer to Him, "Yes." You don't need to say, "Well, you know, if it is according to your will, etc." You just need to believe that the Lord is able and to respond in faith, "Yes."

In Matthew 8:1–3, Jesus cleansed a leper,

When He had come down from the mountain, great multitudes followed Him, and behold a leper came worshipping Him saying, 'Lord, if you are willing, you can make me clean.' Then Jesus put out His hand and touched him saying, 'I am willing. Be cleansed immediately.'" And, his leprosy was cleansed.

Here the question is, "Are You willing to heal?" Jesus said, "I am willing." I believe what the text says. Whatever your illness is, whatever your need is, God is saying, "I am willing." He is able and willing. By faith, we need to believe it.

The third story points out to us that we should never put limitations on what God can do. In Mark 9:14, we see that when Jesus came to the disciples, He had been up on the mountain. Christ had seen a great multitude around them, and some scribes were disputing them. When they saw Him, all the people were greatly amazed and were running to Him and greeting Him. He asked the scribes what they were discussing with the disciples. One in the crowd answered and said, "Teacher, I brought you my son who has a mute spirit. And, whenever it seizes him, it throws him down, he foams at the mouth, and gnashes his teeth, and becomes rigid. So, I spoke to your disciples and asked them to cast it out, but they could not." He answered him and said, "Oh faithless generation, how long shall I be with you? How long shall I bear with you? Bring him to me!" And they brought the boy to Christ, and, when he saw Christ, immediately the spirit convulsed, and he fell on the ground, wallowing and foaming at the mouth. Jesus asked his father, "How long has this been happening to him?" "Often it has thrown my son into the fire and the water to destroy him, but if you can do anything, have compassion on us and help us." Jesus said to him, "If you can! All things are possible to him who believes." Immediately the child's father cried out and said with tears, "Lord, I believe; help my unbelief." Jesus saw the people come running together, and He rebuked the unclean spirit saying to it, "Deaf and dumb spirit, I command you to come out of him and enter him no more." The spirit cried out, convulsed him greatly and came out of him, and the boy became as one dead so that many said he was dead. However, Jesus took him by the hand, lifted him up, and he arose. When he came into the house, his disciples asked Him privately, "Why could we not cast it out?" And He said to them, "This kind can come out by nothing but prayer and fasting." The key here is that, if you believe, all things are possible.

The first story in Matthew 9 was the subject of God's being able. The story in Matthew 8 dealt with God's being willing to heal. And the third story in Mark 9 deals with God's unlimited capabilities. Maybe you have not seen blind eyes gain sight. Maybe you have not seen a lame person who is able to walk. Maybe you have not seen a person live who has been given a sentence of death due to cancer. My dear friends, do not let your lack of experience keep you from believing. Just because you haven't seen it, and just because it hasn't happened to someone you know, doesn't mean God can't do it. It just means you haven't seen it.

If you were to take a recent convert, a person who does not know anything at all about theological treatises or books, etc., and just bring him to the Lord, hand him a Bible, not give him a lot of theological mumbo jumbo, he will come to the conclusion that God is able to heal, God is willing to heal, and God is unlimited in His scope of healing. That's the only conclusion that one can draw from scripture. Often people become confused by trying to learn too many variations or interpretations. We don't need to limit God to what we have or have not seen in our own lives. It becomes a matter of faith.

Jack Deere states in his book, <u>Surprised by the Spirit</u>, "Faith in Jesus' ability to heal is also faith that He does heal." Faith in Jesus' desire to heal is not to be equated with psychological certainty. God will heal when we do not have psychological certainty. In other words, we may not feel like He is going to heal, but

He will because it is based on His authority, on His Word, and what He chooses to do. Faith does not put restrictions on God's ability to act on behalf of His children, for "everything is possible to him who believes."

God heals in respect to His promises. We said in the first place that God heals in relation to our suffering, and that He has compassion toward us. Secondly, we said that God heals according to His glory. Thirdly, we said that God heals in response to our faith. And, finally, we can see that God heals in respect to His promise. Recently, I spoke with a brother in our congregation who has some serious physical problems in his life. He told me that he had been reading James, Chapter 5, all week and that he was ready to come before the elders for prayer.

In James 5:14–16, the scripture reads,

> Is anyone among you sick? Let him call upon the elders of the church, anointing him with oil in the name of the Lord; and the prayer of faith will save the sick, and the Lord will raise him up, and if he has committed any sins, he will be forgiven. Confess your trespasses one to another, and pray for one another, that you may be healed. The effective fervent prayer of a   righteousness man avails much.

So here we see that God is giving the word. God is giving His instruction to the elders in the church. If this weren't part of the life of the Christian church, then God would not have given the instruction. There are some people who believe that just as the Sacrament of Baptism and the Sacrament of Holy Communion should be practiced, praying for the sick and anointing with oil should be a third Sacrament in the church. A major deterrent to this has been the perversion by the Catholic Church many years ago in the Extreme Unction in praying for people who were dying. The scriptures were perverted to pray for people who were dying, even though the original notion and intent of the scripture was praying for the sick to live, and anointing to live, as opposed to anointing to die. Not only did James refer to the elders praying for others, but in the 16th verse, it speaks of us praying for one another, so that we can all pray for one another. It is a directive given in the Word of God that God can and does heal today.

In conclusion, I think we can look at scripture and discover that God does heal today. God is the Sovereign God, and He makes decisions on who should and who should not be healed in accordance with His Sovereign Will, not with the logic of mankind. God uses the wisdom and knowledge that He has given man through medical practices to bring about healing, and God also uses miracles beyond men's logic and reasoning to effect healing. None of the things that we have discussed here today are limited to the first century. They are just as powerful and just as effective today as they were 2,000 years ago, and it is just as reasonable today for God to heal. If healing were a part of the Gospel Message in the first century, then healing is a part of the Gospel Message that we should be preaching today. God heals today.

IS ANY SICK AMONG YOU?

Lee R. Brown

*I*s any sick among you? Let him call for the elders of the church; and let them pray over him, anointing him with oil in the name of the Lord: And the prayer of faith shall save the sick, and the Lord shall raise him up; and if he have committed sins, they shall be forgiven him.   (James 5:14–15)

At the time of James' writing, the time of the apostolic church, or the early church, the most common causes of death were diseases of the body (palsy, leprosy, different plagues, etc.). Everybody had a serious concern and fear of these dreadful, physical culprits. It seemed that no one had a cure for persons stricken with these illnesses.

This is why, in most cases, sick persons were banned from public places; they were oftentimes called "unclean." You may recall that in Old and New Testament times, sick people were not allowed to come near people of royalty, the priest of the temple, nor were they allowed to come in or near the temple of God. Neither new mothers nor their newborn babies were permitted the opportunity of worshipping in the temple until after the time of purification had passed.

It was believed that sickness was the direct effect of a demon- possessed body. Remember the disciples of Christ asking about the man who was born blind, "Master, who did sin, this man, or his parents, that he was born blind" (John 9:2)?

Now Jesus struggles in that same incident to lift the minds of people from believing that direct sin immediately preceded sickness of disease. Jesus answers, "Neither hath this man sinned, nor his parents; but that the works of God should be made manifest in him" (John 9:3).

Illness from natural causes and not from sin was what caused disease in Jesus' day, and what filled people with fear.

Today, one does not have to go far or study long to note and/or name our greatest cause of death in which everybody shares a serious concern. Have you heard anything about the drug problem? The gun problem? The murder problem? The gang problem? The assault problem? The burglary problem? The car theft problem? The juvenile delinquency problem? The carjacking problem? The Black on Black crime problem?

Brothers and Sisters, unlike the sickness in the era of the early church, our society is sick with crime, sick of crime, sick in crime, and sick because of crime. And we have called for the help of many unreasonable antidotes.

Is any sick among you? When three little boys can be killed and cut up like hamhocks, chitterlings, and pig feet, somebody among us is sick!

When grown folk can beat little babies to death because of their crying, and then hide their still bodies in trash dumpsters, somebody among us is sick.

When a 12-year-old elementary student can hold a semi-automatic on an assistant principal, somebody among us is sick.

When persons can drive down the street and shoot and kill innocent people at random, somebody among us is sick.

When preachers preach to their glory, choirs sing to their

glory, and members serve in their glory, and not the glory of God, somebody among us is sick.

In James' day, there were no doctors in most towns or villages; thus, it was the responsibility of the elders of the church to prayerfully apply medicated oil to the body of the ill. Now, the question that many might concern themselves with is, "Do the elders, the preachers, and deacons visit the sick?" Brothers and sisters, our nation is sick. Our state is sick. Our city is sick. Our communities are sick. Even our homes are sick. The people of our community are so sick that one can see the symptoms in the children. Let us take note of some children in America:

Every 95 seconds, a baby is born into poverty.

Every 43 minutes, a baby dies.

Every 2 minutes, a baby is born to a mother who does not attend a church, mosque, or any house of worship.

Every 3 minutes, a baby is born to an unmarried teen mother.

Every 3 minutes, a baby is born to a mother who did not graduate from high school.

Every 6 minutes, a baby is born at low birth weight, weighing less than five and a half pounds.

Every 4 hours, a child is murdered.

Every 11 minutes, a child is arrested for a violent crime.

Every 7 seconds of the school day, a student is suspended from public school.

Every 49 seconds of the school day, a student drops out of school.

In the September, 1994 issue of <u>Memphis Magazine</u>, an article entitled 'The Killing Fields: Can Memphis Save Its Schools?" reports that "In Memphis alone ... the 1993–94 school year saw 87 students suspended for carrying a gun, 183 students suspended for carrying a knife, and 44 suspended for carrying 'other weapons' such as brass knuckles, ice picks, or sharp jewelry ... 283 assaults, 26 of those against school teachers or principals ... 253 fights, 240 reports of 'disorderly conduct,' three rapes, 20 cases of other sexual assaults and 19 'woundings.'"

Is any sick among us? Well, now we see, the sick among us is composed of more than folk in the hospitals. Our children in our public schools are sick. Our brothers and sisters in jail are sick. Our co-workers on our jobs are sick. Our Sunday-go-to-meeting-church-folk are sick. A sick visitation may easily be a stop in the hall of the church between the fellowship hall and the sanctuary.

Is any sick among us? James writes, "Let them call for the elders of the church." Well, our sick brothers and sisters are calling for us. Every church leader in this room represents "the elders of the church." Every minister, every deacon, every trustee, every church school teacher, every annual day chairperson, every president, every advisor, every choir member, every usher, every regular church member can be called a church leader, and every leader represents "the elders of the church."

Brothers and sisters, the **sick among us** are calling for the church. Singing and praying, meeting and eating, and hollering and walloping in our church buildings are not enough. James says, "Pray over them." We must go where the sick folk are. We must take Jesus to the people! The sick are calling for us, but it appears that they will be D.O.A. before we get there.

"Anointing them with oil in the name of the Lord," simply means, whatever it takes to revive this **sick** community, we must do it in the name of the Lord. Social degeneration is a result of spiritual degeneration, and that is a church issue and not a governmental one.

"And the prayer of faith shall save the sick, and the Lord shall raise him up; and if he have committed sins, they shall be forgiven him."

Those of us who feel that our physical illnesses have caused us to be called the "sick among us" should now see that maybe

— 122 —

we should pray "the prayer of faith" for the healing of our "sick" brothers and sisters wherever they might be, and most of the time they are not in the hospital.

> There is a balm in Gilead,
> To make the wounded whole;
> There is a balm in Gilead,
> To heal the sin-sick soul.
>
> Sometimes I feel discouraged,
> And think my work's in vain.
> But then the Holy Spirit
> Revives my soul again.
>
> Don't ever feel discouraged,
> For Jesus is your friend,
> And if you look for knowledge,
> He'll ne'er refuse to lend.
>
> If you can't preach like Peter,
> If you can't pray like Paul,
> You can tell the love of Jesus,
> And say, "He died for all."
>
> There is a balm in Gilead,
> To make the wounded whole;
> There is a balm in Gilead,
> To heal the sin-sick soul.
> ("Balm In Gilead," Traditional)

A CHRISTIAN PERSPECTIVE ON SICKNESS

James M. Coleman

*E*ach one of us sometime or another must face the fact of illness. Our first encounter may be when a family member or close friend is hospitalized. Extensive tests are done; anxious waiting follows until the illness is named. Successful treatment may be the outcome, or it may not be treatable. What is the Christian to do? How is the Christian to react to all that is going on?

There are certain resources with which Christians have to work. These resources are revealed in Holy Scripture. The first resource is that sickness is not nor ever can be ascribed as divine punishment for sin. No person has the right to attribute to God an act that falls in the category of human vengeance, indignation, or retaliation. When people do make such statements, they are making God over in their own image, and it is a despicable image, a misunderstanding of God's love. "For God so loved the world that he gave his only son, that whoever believes in him should not perish but have eternal life" (St. John 3:16). This is God's love, compassionate and sacrificial, that gives life to the world.

The second resource is our own awareness that some illnesses are our own fault. They are the inevitable results of our own actions. Sin, of course, may be a consideration in our illness. Sexual promiscuity invites diseases, some of them causing death. Taking foolish risks with bad weather, being impatient with traffic, overeating or drinking, taking unlawful drugs ... the list could go on and on. Our own self-indulgence is the cause of some sickness that could have easily been avoided except for our own selfishness. We all know when we have, as we say, "tempted fate," and as Christians we should know it clearly. There is an arresting verse in the First Letter of the Apostle Peter,

For what credit is it, if when you do wrong and are beaten for it, you take it patiently? But, if when you do right and suffer for it you take it patiently, you have God's approval. For to this you have been called because Christ also suffered for you, leaving you an example that you should follow in his steps (I Peter 2:20,21).

The third resource is how Christ deals with the sick: He makes them well. The Gospel tells us that "Now when the sun was setting, all those who had any that were sick with various diseases brought them to him; and he laid his hands on every one of them and healed them" (St. Luke 4:40).

St. Matthew records that a paralytic man was brought to him and "seeing their faith, Jesus said to the man, 'Take heart, my son; your sins are forgiven'" (Matthew 9:2). Aren't you surprised? Wouldn't you have expected Jesus to heal him first, and then to absolve him from whatever sin was there? Jesus knows what He must do to save this paralytic.

"Take heart, my son; your sins are forgiven." The implication is that the man is not only paralytic but that he is also morally sick, and before he can be made physically whole he must become spiritually whole. This is the heart of the Gospel. For the fact is that our gospel is a gospel for sinners and for sinners only. Jesus declares emphatically that He has not "come to call the righteous, but sinners to repentance." And when we face the facts about ourselves, we know that we are not whole. St. Paul's declaration that all have sinned may leave us worried and anxious. But when we have examined Christ's scale of priorities, we discover that the first priority is not necessarily physical wholeness. No, the first priority is holiness. This may be upsetting to us and quite disconcerting because of our preoccupation with physical health. Goodness, look at all the money we spend on vitamins and bromides, on health clubs and recreation, in an attempt to find physical wholeness. But Christ's mission is salvation. That involves the redemption not merely of physical and mental illness, but the whole world of creation, physical and spiritual. Christ's concern here with holiness before wholeness brings a confusing realm of priorities to our notice — the divine priorities. He takes a man and exposes him first to divine forgiveness. The depths of that experience we know cannot be plumbed for we are dealing with the mystery of the divine holiness and its standards, and all language to describe it is inadequate. Jesus absolves the paralytic. Then He heals him. Holiness before wholeness is the way Christ deals with the sick. He opens a window into the mystery of cosmic salvation. Put it another way, what you see is what you can see of an iceberg. There is a hidden mountain of God's life and purpose under the surface. We are permitted through His act of healing a glimpse at something of the awesomely vast divine activity of which healing is a part.

Then there is a fourth resource. It is difficult and complex — difficult for me to talk about for you may be reading this in a hospital room, and I am not in the hospital. The fourth resource has to do with how we cope with the suffering that sickness can bring. The testimony through the ages of holy people who have suffered is that God is somehow with them in the suffering. One thinks of Job and Jeremiah. One thinks of the apostle Paul.

In one of his remarkable novels The Gates of the Forest, the Jewish storyteller Elie Wiesel has one of his characters gently reprove his troubled, reserved friend:

> It's inhuman to wall yourself up in pain and memories as if in a prison. Suffering must open us to others. It must not cause us to reject them. The Talmud tells us that God suffers with man. Why? In order to strengthen the bonds between creation and the creator; God chooses to suffer in order to better understand man and be better understood by him. But you insist on suffering alone. Such suffering shrinks you, diminishes you. Friend, that is almost cruel.

"God suffers with man." For us that startling statement should be wonderfully and fearfully real. No exaggeration here, no fantasy run wild. All one has to do is read the Gospels — Matthew, Mark, Luke, and John — and know that God's own divine son, the God-man, died on the cross of Calvary.

But why? The Talmud says, "God suffers with man to strengthen the bonds between creation and the creator and to better understand man and be better understood by him." Yes, yes, I cry as I glimpse Christ in Gethsemane, stand beneath His cross and realize that God knows what it is like to be human and experience how we feel. He hurts the way you and I hurt. Nails tear His flesh, and loneliness breaks His heart. On the cross, He feels our pain.

Love. That is what at bottom strengthens the bonds that link us to God, deepens our understanding. For Calvary is not just another tragedy, the execution of one more innocent man. "God so loved the world that he gave his only begotten son that whoever believes in him should not perish but have eternal life" (John 3:16,17). This, in the last analysis, is why "God suffers with man." Not simply to be understood and to understand. The crucifixion of Christ is an act of love — a love that saves, redeems. It is this that transforms suffering into sacrifice. The God-man not only suffered with us; He suffered for us. "The life

I now live in the flesh," St. Paul explained, "I live by faith in the son of God who loved me and gave himself for me" (Galatians 2:20). It is not sheer crucifixion but crucified love that changed the world, changed you and me, reconciled us to God, made it possible for us to be one with him through faith, with hope and love.

St. Paul was certainly one who knew the blade of difficulty including a physical illness that he described as "a thorn in the flesh." What it was we do not know. He says quite frankly that he prayed to be healed not once but three times and was told "my grace is sufficient for you." St. Paul found Christ in his suffering for it was he who wrote: "Suffering begets endurance. Endurance begets character. Character begets hope, hope that will never be disappointed" (Romans 5:3–5). It was St. Paul who said, "I can do all things through Christ, who strengthens me" (Philippians 4:13).

As Christians, then, we understand that healing is not simply a physical concern. True healing arises in the restored union between the human — body and soul — and God. True healing comes only from God.

HARD TIMES AND ROUGH PLACES

Bill Adkins

*A*s it is written, Behold, I lay in Zion a stumbling stone and rock of offense; and whosoever believeth on Him shall not be ashamed. (Romans 9:33)

When I was a little boy visiting my grandmother in Greenwood, Mississippi, I remember hearing the gospel choir singing in her church, "I'm climbing up the rough side of the mountain." I would visualize that mountain and then see myself climbing it. For some reason that song remains burned in my heart as a foundation of my faith. I've always seen the practicing of my faith as a challenge: meeting one obstacle after another, overcoming the vicissitudes of life and claiming the victory in the name of Jesus. I learned quickly that the rough side of the mountain is the only side you can climb!

God gives us life, but what kind of life? I suggest that our lives are tests, examinations of character and faith. As freewill agents, ours is the choice to challenge or be subdued by the trials of life. Success is a decision that is made, not a condition that just happens. If we look at life as this tremendous examination and challenge, we'll soon realize that our faith is the key to our ultimate victory. I heard someone say that into each life a little rain must fall. Well, it seems like some of our lives are deluged with floods. It was the wisdom of an old woman, my grandmother, who kept reminding me of the challenge that life offers. She would spend hour after hour telling me that storm clouds would gather, but they would eventually go away. She would often sing the old spiritual, "Trouble Don't Last Always." In times of her own trials and tribulations, she would often look up to the sky and repeat the words of the hymn:

> My hope is built on nothing less
> Than Jesus' blood and righteousness.
> I dare not trust the sweetest frame,
> But wholly lean on Jesus' name.
> On Christ the solid rock I stand,
> All other ground is sinking sand.

There are indeed **hard times and rough places** to face in life. Our past, present, and future are cluttered by stumbling stones, obstacles that lay in our way. Dr. Warren W. Wiersbe wrote a beautiful little book entitled The Bumps Are What You Climb On. He maintains that overcoming obstacles and adversities in life is the true test of one's faith. He says,

It is much easier to kick the rock and turn around and go back. The secret to climbing higher is to look away from yourself and your difficulties, and look by faith to Jesus Christ. He knows where you are, how you feel, and what you can do. Turn it all over to Him and start walking by faith. The very rocks that seem like barriers to human eyes will, to the eyes of faith, become blessings.

The overcoming of problems is the seed of Christian testimony. If we only had good times, we would have no testimonies.

It is the act of overcoming that validates the measure of our faith. Christianity is an "overcoming religion." Our belief system is based in victory through Jesus Christ, Our Lord. His victory over death and burial supplies us with the tenet of our faith: **believing**. John 3:16 and Romans 10:9, along with so many other scriptures, support the evidence that our belief in Him is what makes us overcome. The Apostle Paul writes to the Romans that a stumbling stone and rock of offense lay in our way, and that whosoever believeth on Him shall not be ashamed. Paul was concerned that Israel mistook the possession of the law as a means of righteousness. Man will sometimes look to himself and his own intelligence as the solution to all problems. Jesus is the Rock on which we can climb over the adversities of life: health, financial, marital, whatever! We quickly find that faith in ourselves has limits, but faith in Him has no boundaries. All power was given into His hands. In Him we move and breathe and have our very being. Jesus is the Rock on which we climb. I like to use as an illustration this story:

There was once a man who fell down into a deep well. The walls of the well were slippery and wet; he could not climb out. He yelled for help, and along came a fellow. This man looked into the well and saw the predicament and immediately told the man that he couldn't get him out, but he would give him some liquor and drugs to make things easier for him. After the man had used the liquor and drugs, he soon found his sobriety again and began calling for help once more. This time a churchwoman came by. The man cried out, "Please help me out of this well." The woman answered, "I can't get you out of the well, but I'll sit here and read you some scriptures." When the woman had finished, the man realized he was uplifted momentarily, but he was still in the well. Then as the man continued to cry out from the well, a stranger came along the way. The man yelled, "Will someone help me get out of this well?"

The stranger looked at the man and simply said, "I'll get you out." The man in the well said, "But how?" The stranger replied, "You must do exactly as I say." The man agreed and to his amazement, the stranger jumped down into the well with him. The stranger then instructed the man to climb up on his shoulders and get out of the well. The man did this and once upon realizing his freedom looked back into the dark deep well where the stranger now stood. He said, "But how are you going to get out?" The stranger replied, "That's not important. I came so that you could be free!"

Needless to say, Jesus will jump down into the wells of life with you and offer you the opportunity to climb out of your wells upon His shoulders. **Hard times and rough places** are always going to be in our way, but Jesus offers us help and victory through our belief in Him. If you need healing, Jesus is the answer. If you need a financial blessing, Jesus is the answer. If your family is torn apart, Jesus is the answer. We must learn to climb up on the problems of life and claim the victory in the name of Jesus. The old Chinese proverb says, "turn your problems into opportunities." Jesus says, "I am the way, the truth and the life." Paul writes, "I can do all things through Christ, who strengthens me." You must believe in the power of Christ.

The father at the wedding feast at Cana believes ...
The centurion's servant believes ...
Peter's mother-in-law believes ...
The man by the pool at Bethesda believes ...
The palsied man believes ...
The dumb demoniac believes ...

The two blind men believe ...
The man with the withered hand believes ...
The 5,000 He fed believe ...
The Canaanite woman's daughter believes ...
The man at Decapolis believes ...
The son of the widow of Nain believes ...
The man with dropsy believes ...
The woman with the issue of blood believes ...
And the witnesses who saw Him take a walk on a liquid sidewalk believe.

We must believe. No matter what has happened, we must remember that there is no problem too tough for Him. Jesus calls out to us, "Come unto me all ye that are heavy laden and I will give you rest." In the poem "Footprints," the wearied one is lifted by Jesus, and the two sets of footprints in the sand become only one. Jesus will pick you up and carry you through your problem. C.D. Martin and Charles Gabriel said it best when they wrote:

Why should I feel discouraged?
Why should the shadows come?
Why should my heart be lonely?
And long for heaven and home?
When Jesus is my portion,
My constant friend is He.
His eye is on the sparrow,
And I know He watches me.

GOD'S HIGHER PURPOSE

Text: II Kings 5:1–14   Richard D. Sisk

The age-old question still echoes through our minds today. Why does God permit evil and suffering? If God is a loving God, why then does he permit me to get sick? Is my illness some kind of discipline from God? Why are there problems such as sickness and death? Perhaps it has not occurred to us that there is an even greater question that we could ask. If we can't get answers to these weighty imponderables, it may be because we are asking the wrong question. A better question might be: "Does God have a higher purpose in allowing the body to get sick?"

We know intuitively and experientially that if we take care of our bodies through proper diet, rest, and exercise, they will be less likely to become ill. At the same time we realize that in spite of our best precautions, disease can strike, infections can set in, and accidents can happen. So if God allows these kinds of things to occur, and if He is a loving God, then it is logical to assume that He sometimes has a higher purpose in our illness than what is readily apparent.

Tucked away in the fifth chapter of II Kings is a beautiful

illustration of God's higher purpose in healing. The story is that of Naaman, a great warrior of Syria. He is afflicted with leprosy. Upon hearing that there is a prophet in Israel who can possibly cure him, he enlists his king as a liaison to the king of Israel and sets out to procure his healing. When he arrives in Israel, he is sent to the prophet, Elisha. Rather than meeting with Naaman personally, Elisha sends a messenger to tell Naaman that he can be healed if he will simply dip himself in the Jordan River seven times. Naaman's pride is offended, and he refuses to do something so lowly. After his aides prevail with him, Naaman then follows the instructions and is completely cured.

Now I would like to walk through this illustration with you and draw some applications that may speak to your circumstance.

First, I want you see that nothing can make us immune from sickness. We are not invincible, and despite the weight of the popular theology of health and prosperity, bad things do happen to good people. Naaman was a man who had everything a man could want in life. He had professional status. The Bible says that he was a "commander of the army." This means that he held the rank of a general. The word literally refers to a man who is "chief" over many men. In order to achieve this rank, he had to be a warrior among warriors. He had to be tough and physically fit. Sometimes, because of our professional status, we may think we are invincible.

Not only was he a man of professional status, but he was also a man of community standing. The Scripture says that he was "a great man in the sight of his master and highly regarded." The implication is that he was a man with a positive reputation among his peers. Regardless of a man's social standing, illness can bring him down. Infection and accident are no respecters of persons.

In addition to these two, Naaman was also a man of notable success. The Bible says that "through him the Lord had given victory to Syria." He was a man who knew the thrill of victory.

He had marched through the streets of Damascus followed by his captives and his victorious army. However great a man's success may be in the eyes of the world, he can still succumb to illness.

The writer of II Kings tells us next that he was a man of physical strength. Verse one says that he was a "valiant" soldier. The word translated "valiant" is a word that means force and may be translated "strong." He was a man of intimidating physical strength. If physical strength would guarantee immunity from illness, then this man would have never been sick.

Finally, being a soldier, Naaman was a man who served his king and others. There seems to be the feeling that if we serve our fellow man, then we should never become ill. Unfortunately, the very reverse is most often true. In trying to gain acceptance and applause, we can literally make ourselves sick in the service of others.

The development of all of these traits is a noble goal to which we all can aspire. However, no matter how good we are, how strong we are, what position we occupy, or how successful we have been, we can still lose our health. After all of these accolades have been heaped upon Naaman, the introductory verse concludes with the terse statement, "But he had leprosy."

The question for us is not so much the issue of Naaman's healing, but rather how God used his experience of sickness and healing to deal with a more important issue. You see, Naaman's major problem was not leprosy. It was pride. Pride is a far more serious problem, because it deals with a man's character. Pride affects a man's inner self.

Naaman's root problem is seen in the fact that he was unwilling to submit to the "therapy" the man of God offered. He was right in suggesting that the rivers of his own country were cleaner and purer than the Jordan. However, God's directive was to dip in the Jordan. When we let pride keep us from following God's directives, we remain with our problems, even though we can make logical arguments for disobeying God.

His pride is also detected in his reaction to Elisha sending a servant, instead of meeting Naaman in person. He felt that a man of his standing should have a personal audience. Perhaps it was the same feeling you may get when your doctor sends an intern around instead of coming himself. Or perhaps when your pastor doesn't visit you in the hospital, but rather sends another church staff member to visit and pray with you. At any rate, God used this man's illness in order to force him into dealing with another, deeper issue in his life.

While I am not saying that every illness that strikes a person is God's plan to get that person's attention concerning sin in his life, I am saying that every illness is an opportunity for a person to examine his life.

Are there attitudes hidden deep in your life with which you can deal during your illness? Is there bitterness that needs to be surfaced and rooted out? Is pride a problem with you? Do you find it difficult to be obedient to what God may be saying to you? I am convinced that God loves you so much that He is willing to let you suffer in order to make you more like Him.

I am so thankful that God uses means by which to bring about the healing of sickness (in this case Naaman's dipping in the Jordan), but I am also thankful that He uses sickness as a means to deal with other more devastating problems. While you are dealing with your health issues today, I encourage you to let God use your physical problems to help you deal with other issues that affect, but go beyond, your health. God bless you as you discover God's higher purpose.

THE MYSTERY OF HEALING

Burton D. Carley

$\mathcal{F}$or I desire steadfast love and not sacrifice, the knowledge of God, rather than burnt offerings.

(Hosea 6:6)

Go and learn what this means, "I desire mercy and not sacrifice." (Matthew 9:13)

Right from the beginning, there was the possibility of something going wrong. Think about that! Out from the creation pronounced "very good" and into the garden called "delight" the serpent came. This was not the accomplishment of Adam or Eve. The serpent came to them. It came without invitation. Though the world is good and delightful, the world is apparently not perfect.

Yes, things can and do go wrong. According to Ralph Waldo Emerson, there is a crack in everything that God has made. Each of us in our way makes burnt offerings to secure safety. The smoke rises behind our carefully crafted walls, but sooner or later, the cracks appear. So it is that into every life come limitations and heartaches, impairments and losses, handicaps and pains. Without invitation there are burdens to carry and obstacles to overcome. We become aware of our mortality.

It is not easy to face mortality in our society. Offerings are plentiful at the altars of youthful beauty, physical perfection, and self-reliant longevity. Vulnerability is not a quality we seek or admire. Often vulnerability is thought of as something to overcome, a weakness or inferiority. Health and happiness are associated with autonomy and being in control of our body, emotions, and circumstances. From this point of view infirmity causes the loss of dignity. Instead of vulnerability uniting us in a common humanity, we fear that it robs us of our humanity. Some imagine that sickness is a manifestation of evil rather than a natural phenomenon of existence. Certainly we are not encouraged to cultivate the notion of being temporarily well. The need for a physician serves to remind. As Emerson wrote in his journal (1821), "We forget ourselves and our destinies in health, and the chief use of temporary sickness is to remind us of these concerns."

Sickness reminds us of our mortality, our vulnerability, our dependency. We become more aware of what we do not command. We begin to understand why there was the possibility of things going wrong from the very beginning of mythological time. The understanding deepens that life is a process, not a finished thing. It is the nature of life to move, to grow, to change for good and ill. Existence was never all set. The price of our freedom, the price of creativity, the price of eternal possibility, is precariousness. In the process of life we are capable of responding. We have degrees of choice, some influence, but we are not in control. Religion may be thought of as how we respond to what we don't control.

Our very humanity invites us to be religious because

eventually each person must come to terms with his or her limitations, fashioning a response to vulnerability, including mortality as an essential part of identity. In the words of my colleague, F. Forrester Church, "Religion is our human response to the dual reality of being alive and having to die." It is something we must do or become overwhelmed with fear and anxiety that can block us from receiving the grace of each day and opening up to the mystery in which we live and move and have our being.

Part of the mystery is not that things go wrong, but that there is healing and the power of the human spirit that does not allow us to be diminished by disease. By working the reality of limitation and mortality into our understanding, we can achieve a deeper appreciation for what is more beautiful and treasurable. Our transience awakens us to the observation that a person's life consists not in the abundance of things. We begin to learn about the importance of faith, hope, and love. We begin to learn what the prophet meant when he said that God desires mercy and not sacrifice.

It comes as no surprise that Jesus quotes Hosea in defense of his association with the social outcasts of his day. Jesus is not moved by those who feel secure in their righteousness. What moves his heart is suffering. He connects with the vulnerability of others. Healing flows from his compassion, from his ability to identify with the physical, psychological, and social pain of others.

In discussing the healing activities of Jesus, biblical scholar John Dominic Crossan makes a useful distinction between **illness** and **disease**. Both terms signify sickness. **Disease** is what physicians treat when something goes wrong with our biological functions. Medicine seeks a cure for the troubled body. **Illness** is what the patient experiences when well-being is compromised. That experience is much larger than the symptoms of disease. It involves the psycho-social and spiritual dimensions of a person. Feelings of separation and fragmentation are characteristic of illness. Recovery from illness is an act of healing, the experience of balance for harmony or wholeness. The curing of disease is biological in nature. The healing of illness is spiritual in nature.

There are many questions about how the two forms of sickness are related. What is the role of caring, attitude, and belief in medical interventions? To what extent are we responsible for our disease? Why do some people recover quickly while others recover slowly? How do mind, body and spirit work together? There is much we don't know, and this is part of the mystery of healing.

For the cure of disease and the repair of the body we must place our trust in those physicians, nurses, and therapists who practice the varied arts of medicine. For the healing of illness, additional resources are required. That there are resources for healing has been demonstrated by the many people of my congregation who have shared their experience of sickness with me. They provide insights and clues about the mystery of healing. In every instance the working of the human spirit as an agent in the process of healing is related to what I can only identify as connection. To be human is to be connected in relationships. The sources of healing come from these relationships. It is our self-knowledge, and how we are connected to others, and how we are connected to the mystery that holds us all, that allows us to receive healing.

One source of healing flows from insight into oneself, understanding one's own limitations and abilities. I remember a conversation with a member of my congregation. She was receiving treatment for cancer, and a number of things had gone wrong to complicate an already frustrating day in the hospital. As she pondered these events in her empty room, she reflected out loud, "Boy, this is not my day." To her great surprise, a reply was heard. The wise and unsolicited response came from the person mopping the floor outside her door who said, "It never is; you have to make it your day."

We have to make it our day every day regardless of our condition. When we experience misfortune it is easy in the confusion, anxiety, and pain to feel like a victim. Why me? That is the first question. We ask it because we want an explanation; because we want the world to be a place where if we get it right nothing goes wrong; because we believe that sickness is a mistake. So we seek to assign blame to others, to God or fate, or to ourselves.

Why me? It is the most natural question to ask, and it is a trap. It traps our identity by locating it in the unhappy circumstances that come to us. Personhood is a greater thing than any disease. We need not resign responsibility for making our day even in the most compromising circumstances.

The healing question comes after we accept the biblical truth that it rains on the just and the unjust. The healing question is a question of faith. It is not an easy question, but the difficult one of what to do next. What next? It is a question of faith, because faith is how one acts in the world.

It is common to think of faith as a noun, as something possessed. Often it is associated with belief, accepting as reliable and true particular traditions and doctrines. Faith, however, is not a quantity, something that can be measured by our belief. Faith is not a currency for buying what we wish from God. We are not saved from sickness by having "enough" faith. Faith is not a rule or belief for guaranteeing our success, health, or happiness. It does not inoculate us against sorrow or suffering. It does not grant immunity from cancer or heart disease or the many ways sickness can come to us.

Faith is a verb in the Bible. It expresses action. Faith is only as good as what it inspires us to do. The function of faith is not to exempt us from pain, vulnerability, disease, accident, or fear. Rather, faith allows us to meet them and to wrestle from them our humanity. The action of faith is being faithful to everything good and precious available to us in sickness or in health.

Jesus once came across a man who had been blind from birth. The disciples were curious because it was believed that suffering was the result of sin. "Rabbi," they asked, "who sinned, this man, or his parents that he was born blind?" Their teacher said that they were asking the wrong question. Disability is not punishment. It is an inevitable part of the human experience. Guilt and self-hatred are misplaced. The question is not one of blame but one of response. The healing response moves from cause to purpose. What does my situation have to teach me? That is the right question.

Acceptance is an act of faith. Seeking what our situation can teach us is an act of faith. Healing begins with the acknowledgment that while we have choices, we are not in control. Knowledge of our limitations and abilities connects us to the world as it is where we are challenged to make each day our day. The mystery of healing is that we have more resources for meeting that challenge than we ever imagined.

A second source of healing is our connection to others. I remember a conversation with a member of my congregation. When diagnosed with AIDS, he began facing the difficult task of working through the confusion and anger and fear of his life being completely changed. The important thing is that he decided not to do this alone. He asked, "Does God send AIDS to people?"

I responded, "Not the God I worship." Hearing no judgment, the defenses came down. This is what happens when we accept vulnerability, ours and others. We become available to be touched. He began to share his sense of grief, of loss. We cried and we laughed, and did so on many occasions. It is one of the most healing things we can do when we are in pain or with someone who is in pain. It is a simple thing, and that is to let our pain be pain and to share it.

It is a simple thing and a difficult one. Why is it so difficult to share what hurts us? Perhaps we do not want to be associated with chronic complainers, not only because they are so toxic, but also because they tend to drive away the very sources of comfort they seek. Perhaps we feel that our painful feelings will be too intense or burdensome for those we truly care about. Perhaps we want to protect the people we are intimate with. Perhaps we believe that talking about pain does not help anything or change anything. Perhaps we feel that showing vulnerability is the blood that alerts the human sharks to the presence of prey. Perhaps we fear that in openly recognizing painful feelings we will be overwhelmed by them. Perhaps we give in to the natural tendency to want painful events to be over and done with. Perhaps we are insecure about admitting that unpredictable events can unfold about us. Perhaps we are fearful that self-exposure will lead to humiliation, that those with whom we share our vulnerability will not take it seriously.

It is difficult, and we should remember that Job refused to bear his pain in silence. Likewise, it is good to remember that the Psalmists gave public voice to their laments. It is instructive to remember that Jesus cried out from the pain of the cross, "My God, My God, Why have you forsaken me?" By sharing painful feelings with a trusted companion, we don't cover up or minimize our wounds. It is only in refusing to retreat in privacy with difficult feelings that we are able to accept them and move through them to new possibilities. In sharing our burdens, healing takes place. Or as Marion Woodman put it, "God comes in through the wounds."

"I require mercy, not sacrifice," we are told. We are asked to consider what this means. Does not mercy move beyond judgment while sacrifice remains rooted in judgment? Mercy suggests acceptance, the ability to offer blessing without demanding perfection. Sacrifice suggests that acceptance is the result of an arrangement. Rather than being an act of love freely given, blessing is the reward earned by fulfilling certain conditions. The burden of sacrifice is that it keeps score. Mercy lets go of the score and moves toward compassion. Compassion is the great conduit that brings us into contact. Literally, compassion means to suffer with. We cannot earn compassion nor do we really give it to one another. It is the recognition of what is shared, the mutual vulnerability of being human. There is a healing quality in feeling a part of one another, connected rather than isolated in our pain.

We are required to practice mercy, not sacrifice. Whenever we allow pain to be pain and share it with others, or listen to the pain of others, we are doing holy work. In those moments the depth of friendship, love, and intimacy is known. It is truly knowledge of God. The mystery of healing is that God comes through the wounds.

A third source of healing is our connection to the mystery that holds us all. I remember a conversation with a member of the congregation. She was endowed with a generous intellect, and she used it well in a productive academic career. She understood the world through the mind of a scientist, and did not pretend to be religious by conventional standards. Advanced in age and suffering from an advanced disease, she calmly decided to "cooperate with the inevitable" as she put it. The last weeks of her life were spent at home with the help of Hospice.

During my last visit she spoke with profound gratitude about her life. Though weak in body, her spirit was peaceful and suffused with joy. She said, "I've been thinking about my life, about how quite remarkable it is. It has been filled with so many wonderful and interesting people. There were so many opportunities given to me. I loved my travels, and I gave witness to the beauty of the earth. What blessings! Even now, I am receiving such care and love." I knew her life had not been free of tragedy. She did not deny that tragedy. The tragedy was accepted as was the fact that the good life is not one exempted from trouble, suffering, and deep sorrow.

At the end of the visit, after she had given a full accounting of the people and things and events she felt so blessed by, I told her that she couldn't fool me. She was a deeply religious person, I asserted, because she understood that life is a precious gift we have not earned, and that the important thing is to pay attention to the grace of it in times of gladness and sorrow, to appreciate it even as we lose it. With that unexpected confirmation, delight flashed from her tired eyes.

When sickness comes and things go wrong, the difficulty of the moment may lead to a kind of amnesia, a forgetfulness. Our focus narrows to the trouble at hand, and we become separated from the larger life that holds our own. Clinging to what we don't want to lose, we forget that giftedness of being here in the first place. We fail to remember all the opportunities and blessings we have enjoyed. We stop expressing thankfulness in prayer or contemplation. We neglect to observe the ordinary gifts available in sickness and health. We need to awake once again to a way of seeing expressed in these lines from the poem "To Earthward" by Robert Frost, "Now no joy but lacks salt/That is not dashed with pain/And weariness and fault."

We don't deserve most of the hard things that come to us. We also don't deserve the wonder and beauty of the sun rising in the morning. It is only there for us to appreciate. The glory of it all is that through our gladness and sorrow we are connected to this creation and the power that sustains it. There is so much we do not understand, probably most of everything. So it is best to face earthward, and ground ourselves in the humus where humility and humor dwell. There, in that place, down low, we are divested of all grandiosity. There we remember that from dust we came and to dust we return. We remember, like Job, "Naked I came from my mother's womb and naked I will depart." We remember, not in resignation, but in joy. Feeling connected to the larger reality is a source of healing. Healing comes in appreciation and gratitude, in giving worth (worship) to the Mystery as something beyond measure. It is a way of acknowledging that creation does not belong to us; rather, we belong to it. We are the strangers and sojourners here. Only God is at home.

At the end of healing, at the end of everything, can only be praise. Through praise, we are transformed. The great poet Rainer Maria Rilke understood this so well in the following poem translated by Albert Ernest Flemming:

> O tell us, poet, what it is you do?
> — I praise.
> But in the midst of deadly turmoil, what
> Helps you endure, and how do you survive?
> — I praise.
> And that which nameless is, anonymous,
> How do you, poet, still call out to them?
> — I praise.
> Who grants you your right to pose in any guise,
> Wear any mask, and still remain sincere?
> — I praise.
> And that the stillness and the violence —
> Like the star and storm — know and acknowledge
> you?
> —because I praise.

How do we endure in a world where things go wrong, in a world where we are aware of being alive and having to die, in a world we do not control? We do so by being open to the sources of healing given to us regardless of how things go wrong. This is the greatest mystery of healing — that it is built into the nature of things. Healing comes to us in our connect-edness to self, others, and the Mystery. Healing shines forth out of the human spirit where in our deepest struggle with mortality, there is the possibility of joy and praise.

KEEP ON BELIEVING

Text: Mark 5:21–43   Kimberly Campbell

$\mathcal{M}$aster storyteller and author Madeline L'Engle, in her version of the gospel story called The Glorious Impossible, begins her story with the angel Gabriel's visit to the Virgin Mary.

An angel came to Mary. A 14-year-old girl was visited by an angel, an archangel. (In Scripture, whenever an angel appears to anyone, the angel's first words usually are, 'FEAR NOT!' — which gives us an idea of what angels must have looked like.)

"Fear not!" We've become accustomed to hearing that exclamation as a prelude to divine intervention. That is, as a signal that God has done, or is about to do, something marvelous. Recall the angel appearing to the shepherds in the field, announcing the birth of the Christ Child in Bethlehem; or Jesus calling out to his disciples as he walked on the water toward their boat; or the angel who greeted the women as they peered into Jesus' empty tomb.

In the Mark 5 text we have yet another "fear not!" As we encounter a desperate father whose last ditch-effort at saving his daughter's life has failed. His anguish is met with bad news. It's too late. She's already dead. Why trouble the teacher any further? But that's not the last word, for Jesus answers the announcement of death with **"fear not"**— literally **let go of your fear** — and he encourages Jairus to "keep on believing." Jairus' worst fears have been realized, yet Jesus boldly challenges him to exercise his faith even in the face of a lost cause. Imagine Jesus calling him to faith in his darkest hour, to hope when all hope is lost.

I wonder what went through the mind of Jairus? Or the minds of those from his household who were in the awful position of being the bearers of bad new? Frustration, perhaps? They had, after all, witnessed the girl's sudden decline and her father's agony. Why would Jesus now prolong the agony by giving him false hopes?

The girl is dead, Teacher. We've all got to face it. Glossing it over and reinforcing denial isn't going to help Jairus come to terms with his loss. This is a reasonable man. He exhausted every resource, conventional and unconventional, just to restore his daughter to health. When he heard you were coming, knowing your reputation as a miracle-worker and healer, he fell down at your feet and begged for your help. He was willing to cast aside all personal pride and public image in coming to you, Jesus. Now don't bring him to shame again by asking him to keep on believing. Let it rest.

Would their frustration have been mixed with disappointment? Jesus, here you are on an urgent mission, responding to a 911 with a child near death, and you allow yourself to be interrupted by a woman in the crowd — an unclean woman at that! Surely you know the law says she must be left alone when in that condition. Then, with the crowds pressing in on you, you actually stop to ask, "Who touched me?" Look, Jesus, if you are ever going to succeed in this business, you're going to have to get some priorities. Let the little stuff go. "Who touched me?" Was that woman so important that a little girl's life had to be sacrificed over a point of clarification? Look, we all placed a lot of confidence in you, thinking you'd appreciate the gravity of the situation. ...

Frustration and disappointment are common feelings among believers. We come in good faith to Jesus with all of our best hopes and prayers, and our expectations go unfulfilled. We pray for healing, and the condition worsens. We pray for deliverance, and we go from the frying pan into the fire. We pray for peace, and chaos continues to reign. Yet, in spite of all that, in spite of our seemingly ineffective faith, Jesus calls each one of us to "give up our fear" and "keep on believing," as he goes with us into our darkest situations, just as he went with Jairus.

To what kind of belief does Jesus call us? What kind of faith is required? Perhaps the answer lies in the story that interrupts the story of Jairus' daughter. The inserted story serves more than one purpose. One obvious purpose is that it builds suspense. Will Jesus make it on time? Will the girl hang on? The story within a story also serves as interpretation. There is a sense in which the way the unclean woman approaches Jesus is an illustration of the kind of faith to which we are called, even if it is growing faith.

Jesus had been crisscrossing the Sea of Galilee, going from Gentile to Jewish territory, teaching, healing, and performing miracles. His wonder-working reputation had rapidly spread throughout the region, so that when he landed back in Jewish territory, he was met at the beach by a great crowd of curious onlookers. Not all were just thrill-seekers, however, as we have already seen in Jairus. His coming to Jesus was very purposeful. There is also this woman who had been suffering from hemorrhages for 12 years. Levitical law instructs that a menstruating woman is considered unclean, and that anyone who touches her is defiled. So by law, the woman had lived for at least 12 years in total isolation, an outcast in the eyes of friends, family, neighbors, and the synagogue.

The author tells us that she had spent everything she had to find a cure; she had tried virtually everything, and she had only gotten worse. With time running out, she secretly approaches Jesus. Pushing her way through the crowd, she comes to Jesus from behind, just within arm's reach. The author discloses the woman's thoughts: "If I but touch his clothes, I will be made well." While this sounds for all the world more like superstition or magical thinking than real faith, Jesus recognizes it as living faith, however immature. Faith in any degree is still faith. Jesus recognizes the difference in the moving throng between a push and a touch, between an onlooker and a true seeker.

When the woman touches Jesus' garment, she is instantly healed. The author leaves no doubt in our minds that her physical healing is immediate and complete, and that the woman is aware of this. Jesus feels the power go out from him, and he stops and looks for the one who touched him. "But the woman, knowing what had happened to her, came in fear and trembling, fell down before him, and told him the whole truth." Most assuredly, that took courage. She came in fear and trembling not only because she had been found out, but because she was painfully aware that, in conventional thought, for her to touch Jesus in her condition was to defile him. Imagine the horror of the crowds who had also come into contact with her as she pushed past them to reach Jesus. The inescapable modern parallel is someone with AIDS coming into the church to find an accepting community, a place of healing, comfort, and belonging, only to be confronted with the fears and prejudices, and therefore the rejection of the very people who should have extended welcome in the name of the Lord.

Yet, this stigmatized woman comes clean. She comes forward and, falling down before Jesus, she tells the whole truth. How interesting that the text doesn't say, "She explained herself." Instead, "She told him the whole truth." The woman models the act of confession, which is not just explaining ourselves, offering justifications or excuses. It is telling the truth, the whole truth, the inner truth. Confession is to tell of our need of Jesus, to realize our unworthiness, to come to terms with our inability to heal or to change ourselves, and to open ourselves to the greater power of God.

The woman's confession was not the end of the story, however. Jesus' intent was not to expose her but to bless her. She reaches only to touch his hem from behind. He makes his face to shine upon her. "Daughter, your faith has made you well; go in peace, and be healed of your disease." In that crystalline moment, Jesus legitimized her by naming her as one of his own ("daughter"), received her gesture of faith, healed her body, and restored her to the life of the community. Her healing was complete.

Jesus seeks to bring us not to a quick fix in life, but to completion and wholeness. The abundant life that he offers us is not a life that we reform or shape up out of our own resources; it is a life transformed by the regenerating power of Jesus Christ. It is life given to us anew. Could it be that this is the lesson Jesus is trying to teach Jairus and the disciples as he takes them into the house filled with mourners? Is the raising of the little girl from the dead intended as a parable of what must happen to us if Jesus is to bring us into fullness of life? Could it be that we may have to go through the valley of deep darkness (shadow of death) before we can be brought into the light of new life in Christ? Even then, we shall fear no evil, for the Lord is with us, comforting us, offering hospitality in the midst of hostility, anointing and blessing us, and filling our cup to overflowing.

The professional mourners have already arrived on the scene and have begun their loud weeping and wailing, giving expression to the grief of the household. Jesus confronts their exaggerated display, "Why do you make a commotion and weep? The child is not dead but sleeping." They laugh at him. (In truth, so do we. It does not soften the blow of death to call the casket room at a funeral home the "slumber room." We all know better, and euphemism adds insult to injury.) He puts the laughing mourners outside and takes the child's mother and father and the three disciples with him into where the child is laid out. He takes her by the hand and says, "Little girl, time to get up," like a loving father

— 153 —

gently waking his child in the morning. To everyone's amazement, she immediately gets up and begins walking around. Jesus, still the nurturing parent, sees to it that she is given something to eat.

"Let go of your fear" and "keep on believing." How can we do that? How can we have faith in the face of our lost causes and continue to hope when all hope is lost? Because we have in Christ one who has already gone before us through the valley of deep darkness, who was obedient even unto death, and who entrusted all outcomes into the hands of a loving God. And on the third day, the God of the universe entered into that tomb of death and darkness, took Jesus by the hand and said, "My son, it's time to get up. The night is over. It's a new day."

We know that Jesus commands the powers of the universe so that even the winds and the seas obey him. We know that he has authority over the powers of evil and that demons fear him. But what has he to do with the complexities of human life? This story demonstrates a warm, accessible, human Jesus who is well-acquainted with the pain and the need of our humanity, and whose compassion and grace know no bounds. Because of that, we can approach him with confidence that our faith, however immature, will make us whole. Because of that, we can face our darkest moments, knowing that God is with us in them. Because of that we can also have faith enough to enlarge the circle of inclusion in the Christian community so that the grace of Jesus Christ is extended to **all persons** without distinction.

The nameless woman needed a kind of healing that the world could not give. She received a wholeness that was beyond comprehension. Jairus came seeking healing for his daughter. He was shown the way to new life by the one who is Life itself, the one who calls us today to "let go of your fear" and "keep on believing."

HEAL THE SICK

Text: Matthew 10:7,8a   Alfred DeWayne Hill

*V*ery little is heard or said about "healing" among mainline Protestant denominations. This is largely due to the charlatans and quacks. These are the impostors, who pervert and misrepresent the true tenets of the Biblical command to heal the sick. They do so by portraying themselves as agents of divine healing. Their magical performances, laden with both trickery and fraud, are designed to swindle human emotions from vulnerable audiences. It is these theatrics that have caused this very pensive, consequential, and serious decree of our Lord to meet with quiet but sure, certain, and obstinate rejection. At the root of the problem is the sad picture of people on street corners, beguiled, delirious, and confused humanity who await the touch of a healing hand — the pronouncement of some mystical words — that will grant them release from some illness, and then result in shouting, testimonials, or some comical behavior.

Despite our obvious refusal to comply and obey the instructions of scripture, there is both a place and purpose for this most sacred, endearing, and much needed ministry in the life of the Church. "Too often," wrote two physicians, Frank B. Minirth,

M.D., and Paul D. Meier, M.D., "there is a tendency to place faith and science in opposition to each other instead of joining them" (Happiness is a Choice, p. 7). Jesus saw this union, for he charged his followers with the command, "Heal the sick."

From what is dictated by scripture, it is evident to me that the church's faithfulness to respond to the call to a healing ministry requires a holistic definition of what it means to be sick. What do we mean when we say, "I am sick" or "He (or she) is sick" or even, "The child is sick." It is both commonplace and ancient, for the experience of illness, pain, and suffering is akin to the human drama. It knows neither race nor class; illness, like death, is a great equalizer.

The carpenter of Nazareth used this common reference in one of his many parabolic utterances as a window so that the light of the kingdom's truths might shine through. "I was sick and you visited me." David heard this remark from an Egyptian servant who replied to an important question, "My master left me, because three days ago I fell sick." After Nathan, the prophet, departed from David, "The Lord struck the child that Uriah's wife bare unto David, and it was very sick." Thomas Nashe used these same words in his remembered work, "Adieu! Farewell Earth's Bliss!":

> Brightness falls from the air;
> Queens have died young and fair;
> Dust hath closed Helen's eyes,
> I am sick, I must die,
> Lord, have mercy on me.

This is an important inquiry when we consider Jesus charged with this arduous, weighty, and compulsory imperative. Jesus gave it to persons who were trained physicians. Indeed the field of medicine was well established during the Master's time. It owed its existence to the Egyptian, named Imhoptep, a brilliant, scholarly, and astute genius. He was said to have written the now famous Edwin Smith Papyrus — the oldest document on surgery, believed to have been recorded as early as 4200 or as late as 3100 B.C. But there is no evidence to indicate that those who accepted Jesus' invitation, "Follow me and I will make you fishers of men," had read these papers, graduated, did any internship nor completed any residency to be considered physicians.

But the fact that Jesus empowered those who were not physicians to engage in a ministry of healing, is evidence of the broadness of his own definition of "sickness." One can see this wide, expansive, and immense understanding of what it means to be sick in the New Testament's word for "sick." The Greeks used the term, "asthenes," which is the same term for "weak." Twenty-six times this word appears in the New Testament. It is the same term that Paul used when he wrote to the Romans, "Strength is made perfect in weakness," and, "Weak is faith," or "Bear the infirmities of the weak"; and to the Corinthians, "Many are weak," "To the weak I became weak that I might win the weak," and "When I am weak, then I am strong." So when Jesus said, "Heal the sick," he was saying "Heal the weak ones," for this is what the literal Greek says when it reads, "asthenountas Terapeuete." Literally, it says, "Ailing (ones), heal ye" or in other words, "Heal the weak ones."

Here is the reason for the limited attention given by the Church to this ministry of healing and for the Church's choice to leave the total burden of healing to those who practice medicine or to those attention seekers, who masquerade in the illicit, deceptive and hypocritical garments of religious sanctimony that draws and allows sincere and earnest people to place their hopes, even destinies in the hands of counterfeit and non-rewarding systems and practices. Our definitions and understanding of what it means to be sick are far too narrow, localized, restricted, and even prejudicial. We see the world of weakness from our own backyards, and the ground in them is so little and hard, stubborn and cold that you can't plant a row of anything, only one tomato, one okra, one squash, and pepper at a time. What we need is a transplant of our spiritual eyes so that our spiritual capacities for seeing, feeling, and understanding can become wider and deeper.

Consider that it is the failure of the church to enlarge its definition of what it means to be sick that has limited the scope and
nature of the church's work. We can see this in the all-important
question, "Who are the weak ones?" Certainly, Jesus was confronted with them, persons who were spindly, forceless, and ineffective. The woman who had the issue of blood and the man who
laid at the pool for 38 years, awaiting the mysterious troubling of
the water. Who can forget Peter's mother-in-law who was sick
with fever in the house? Jesus' encounter with a man who was so
severely weakened that he was lowered by friends through a
neighbor's rooftop into the midst of a house where Jesus was
teaching? All of these were victims of physical maladies that rendered them weak, emasculated, and ineffectual, devoid of much
needed strength to properly stand, walk, talk, and even see.

But is weakness only a physical phenomenon? Is it reserved
for only that aspect of our human economy that relates to limbs
that can be broken or to immune systems that come under attack
from life-threatening diseases or to this capacity for seeing that
can be ruptured, that can send even a blind Batimaeus into an
experience with the night's shadows, whose morning of light
never comes? Far too often, this has been how we Christians have
understood this extent of living, as a dysfunction of our biological
chemistry. What has resulted from this narrowness has been a
concern with illness in the church that has not extended beyond
visitations to hospitals and convalescent homes, sending and
receiving get well cards and flowers, and prayer.

And when I consider that Jesus did not provide those whom
he charged with the responsibility of healing the sick with a list of
illnesses, this is for me a revelation that the weak ones are not
merely that woman with an issue of blood or that man who sat at
the pool for 38 long years. What of the brother who did not leave
home and who not would join in the welcoming celebration of his
prodigal brother? What of that rich young ruler who went away
sorrowful when told to sell what he had and give it to the poor?
And what of that woman of Samaria, whom Jesus met at the well,

whose life had been torn asunder by moral and ethical impropri-
ety? Together, these affirm that people need not only to be healed
in body, but also in mind, soul, and spirit. Maybe, this is one of the
reasons David A. Seamands' book <u>Healing for Damaged
Emotions</u> has sold 750,000 copies. People are not only weak physically; they are weak emotionally and spiritually.

We must enlarge our definitions of sickness because weakness
is not limited to mortal houses that are made out of clay. Persons
can be weak emotionally and spiritually as well as physically. The
future depends upon this enlargement of our definitions of what it
means to be sick because it has been proven that there is an illness
in this land that cannot be eliminated either by new and better
jobs, affordable housing, or by education or mere elected public
officials. It is a weakness of the man's spirit, soul, and mind that
leads to damaged emotions, low self-esteem, depression and guilt,
resentment and envy, even perfectionism, inability to trust or
believe in one's self, one's neighbor, and one's God. When one is
not delivered from this, it can result in the destruction of one's
body with drugs, alcohol — but even more — murder, rape, and
robbery. The Church must accept this mandate: "Heal the sick."

Consider, finally, that we have been provided with the tools
and means to be agents of healing. Jesus gave to us tools when he
instructed the disciples, "Heal the sick." He then followed with,
"And preach as you go, saying the kingdom of heaven is at hand."
This is a participle that means, "As you are going — healing, raising the dead, cleansing lepers, and casting out demons — preach
that the kingdom of heaven is at hand." Don't do one without the
other, for the evidence of one is in the other and the tool to accomplish one is in the other. When the kingdom of heaven is pro-
claimed, the weak one will be healed, and the instrument needed
to heal these weak ones is proclamation.

And I am delighted and glad that this is all that Jesus left to
heal the sick because this allows me to know that I don't need to
compete with the medical industry, placing faith and religion in
opposition to science. The two of them are not enemies, but

partners working together, for "every good and perfect gift" comes from God. God gave us science, and from it has come hospitals, doctors, nurses and much more. But also, God gave us faith, the Church, the Word, the Holy Spirit, the preacher, and more. The two are not in competition with each other. One writes a prescription for medicine to heal the body; the other writes a prescription for what can heal the soul, mind, and spirit. While one is needed for the diseases of the body, the other is needed for those habits, thoughts, and lifestyles that can lead to those diseases of the body.

Jesus said, "As you are going, preach the kingdom of heaven." Here is the Church's instrument for healing. What a pity we think so lightly of the Word! Yes, words can injure, wound, inflict pain, and even destroy, for what child can stand as evidence of what an unmeasured, ill thought, ugly, distasteful, uncomplimentary, unkind, and humiliating word can do to one's sense of worth and appreciation of one's self. The childish adage, "Sticks and stones may break my bones, but words can never hurt me," is untrue. Words can hurt, injure, damage, and destroy. Let a child hear repeatedly that he or she is nothing, and that child will prove the prophecy true.

But if words can injure, then words can heal. Jesus knew this to be true, for he married "proclamation" to healing the sick. And this marriage must never be annulled if the sick among us are to be healed. So let us proclaim the Word for in it is the promise that the brokenhearted can be healed, the enslaved can be set free, and the weak can be made strong. Proclaim the Word; for in it they that wait upon the Lord shall be renewed. The low can be lifted. The crooked will be made straight. The diseased can be cured. The guilty can be pardoned, and the lost will be found. The lonely will find a friend; the broken can be made whole; the blind can see; the corrupt can be cleansed; the foolish can be made wise; the misguided can find direction; and the sad can be made glad.

THE SCANDAL OF THE CROSS:
HOW TO ENDURE EVIL WITH LOVE

David M. Knight

One of the greatest scandals of Christianity is that Jesus did not come to take away pain.

In the Scriptures and in the Eucharistic celebration, Jesus is presented as the "Lamb of God who takes away the sin of the world" (John 1:29). But nowhere does it say that He takes away all pain.

This makes us wonder just what kind of Savior Jesus is. Does He save us only from the consequences of sin after death — from everlasting condemnation — or does He also save us from the terrible effects the sins of the world have on our lives here on earth?

Does Jesus save us here and now from the evils of war, crime, drug abuse, oppression, slander, sickness, famine, and death?

Does Jesus save us from drunken drivers and crazy snipers, from rapists and terrorists?

What does Jesus do to straighten out our environment, to make the world safe for those who just want to live normal lives and raise happy families? Is Jesus a Savior of life, liberty, and the pursuit of happiness?

The answer, of course, is that He is — but not in the way we expect.

Jesus doesn't tell His disciples just how He is going to go about saving the world until halfway through the Gospel — and then not until they profess unconditionally their faith in Him as Messiah (Matthew 16:13–28).

The reason for this condition is that Jesus did not match the job description of the Messiah that was current in Israel. He wasn't going to be the kind of Savior they expected — and all human beings naturally expect. So first they had to accept Him unconditionally in faith as the Messiah, then He could tell them what kind of Messiah He was actually going to be.

What He told them — in a nutshell — is that He would save the world by enduring evil with love. And anyone who accepts Jesus as Savior and wants to enter into the salvation He gives must also be prepared to endure evil with love. "If a man wishes to come after me, he must deny his very self, take up his cross, and begin to follow in my footsteps" (Matthew 16:24).

This is what it means to carry the cross: to endure with love that portion of the world's evil that happens to fall upon us. To share in the redemption of the world — both as receiving that redemption for ourselves and as helping to extend it to others — means to endure with love those consequences of sin in the world that cause pain and suffering in our own lives.

Jesus does not save us from evil by stamping out evil with force — or with His divine power as God. His effort as Savior does not go into cleaning up the environment. He doesn't save us as human beings by changing what is outside of us — not even by preventing other human beings from doing things to us. He saves us by changing our hearts, by empowering us to change in the very depths of our being — in mind and heart and will. He saves us, essentially, by empowering us to love like God.

This is true salvation. It is not salvation just to be delivered from pain or temptation. If Jesus stamped out sin on earth, imposed a reign of peace and justice, and established a society based on authentic values; if He purified our human environment of all falsity and deception, of all bad example and enticement to evil; if He got rid of drugs, alcohol abuse and crime, pornography and manipulative advertisement, and stopped all wars and oppression — how would that make us any different?

In the absence of temptation we might not sin as much as we do now, but would we ourselves really be radically different? We are not saved by changes outside of ourselves, but by a change in what we are, a change on the level of our hearts and minds and wills. And this is the change to which Jesus invites us, the change His grace can accomplish in us if we accept it.

This is where faith comes in. Is it really possible to endure evil with love? Is it possible to love back when we are being tortured? Robbed? Raped? When a loved one is killed before our very eyes? When someone gets our son or daughter addicted to drugs? When we are maimed for life by an irresponsible, drunken driver?

"No," we spontaneously answer. "We can endure these things if we have no choice, and perhaps endure them without giving in to hatred. But to endure them with love — to love back in response to such evil — is just not humanly possible. It cannot be done."

And yet Jesus did it. What is humanly impossible can be done. It can be done, not just by God, but by any human being who shares in the life of God. And this is what grace is: a sharing in the life of God.

Jesus came to save us by offering us a share in the life of God. God's life is essentially knowing and loving, but above all it is loving. The scriptural definition of God is simply "God is love" (I John 4:7, 8). If we share in God's life, we can love as God does. If we love as God does, we must be sharing in His life. This is what salvation is all about.

If we love as God does, nothing can harm us. This is the sense in which, yes, Jesus does come to save us from all that menaces our existence, from all that threatens to diminish our lives here on earth.

In one of the passages in which He predicts suffering on the cross for His disciples, Jesus says an apparently contradictory thing. "They will manhandle and persecute you," He says, "and some of you will be put to death." Then He concludes, "Yet not a hair of your head will be harmed" (Luke 21:12–18). How can Jesus make two such statements in the same breath?

The answer is that nothing can harm us except that which causes us to hate. If we are robbed and we turn into haters, if we are raped or tortured or just betrayed by a friend and it causes us to live the rest of our lives in hatred, then, yes, we have been harmed. But if we are robbed and we love back, raped and we love the rapist, tortured or betrayed and we respond with love for the one who is afflicting us, then we have not been harmed. Our lives have not been diminished but enhanced, because we have been enhanced. We have become more like God.

Jesus teaches that the fullness of life, authentic liberty, and the only effective pursuit of happiness in this world all come down to one thing: learning to love as God does means enduring evil with love, loving back with the fullness of His love in response to everything that is.

The doctrine of the cross presupposes the doctrine of grace. Without the gift of sharing in God's own life, God's own act and power of loving, what Jesus says about taking up our cross and enduring evil with love would just be absurd. It is humanly impossible. But it is possible for those who can love divinely, and this is what grace empowers us to do.

This is what salvation is all about. Not everyone will accept Jesus as Savior on these terms. And all of us will be at least tempted to insist, as people did in Jesus' own time, that Jesus "come down from that cross" as a condition for believing in Him (Matthew 27:40).

"What use," our minds argue, "is a savior who cannot save? And what does it mean to be 'saved' if one is not delivered from pain and suffering in this world?" When the human tragedies of death, injustice, sickness, or just moral mediocrity on earth become overwhelmingly real to us, Jesus as Savior may seem unreal.

If we are going to grow in our ability, not only to accept Jesus as Savior, but to rejoice in the salvation He gives, and even to embrace the cross with love, then there are four things we should keep in mind:

First, God does not send suffering to us, but He does allow it to happen. People often get the idea that Jesus wants everyone to have a cross, that this is part of God's plan for the world.

The answer to this is that God doesn't want anyone to suffer.

Some pain is part of God's creation; there are natural forces that cause sickness, pain, and suffering. But whatever the reason for them, or however they came about, God wants us to find the way to neutralize them so that no one will ever suffer from them again. The elimination of pain is one of the great projects God calls upon the human race to work on in love.

Other sufferings — and these are the worst — are caused by people's failure to love one another. When people sin against us, or we against them, this causes pain that is the direct result of sin.

This pain God never wills, never desires to happen. But He could not prevent it without taking away human freedom. The real problem about evil in the world is not a problem about evil; it is a problem about freedom. The question is not, "Why does God allow bad things to happen?" but "Why did God create us free?" If we accept to be free and able to love, then we have to accept the consequence that people will also be able to sin and to hurt one another.

The second thing to keep in mind is that Jesus does not promise to spare His followers pain, but He does promise it can never harm us.

Jesus does not grant a kind of immunity to those who believe in Him, so that their children will never get sick, their businesses will never fail, they will not get hurt in automobile accidents, wars, or earthquakes. If He did this, the world would be full of profiteering Christians who know what side their bread is buttered on. What Jesus promised is to give us the grace to turn every evil into good by loving back in response to it.

A third thing to be conscious of is that our feelings do not diminish our love. It is not always possible, even with the fullness of grace, to feel love and forgiveness for another. We may feel like killing someone who has hurt us. We may, on the feeling level, want that person to die a slow death in torment. But love is in the will.

Our love is measured, not by our feelings, but by what we choose to desire, by the desires we insist on claiming as our own. For this our model is Jesus in His agony in the garden; there He did not feel like going to the cross. He just kept repeating to the Father, "not my will but yours be done" (Luke 22:42).

Finally, to "endure evil with love" can mean two things: it can mean that we ourselves love back in response to evil. It can also mean that we endure evil with the help of the love we receive from others. Jesus calls us to "endure evil with love," in both of these senses. He does not want anyone to carry the cross alone. He Himself supports us, and He wants us to support one another.

If the salvation Jesus offers is a call to "endure evil with love," then it is a call to carry our cross with the help and support of others who love us, and it is a call to help others carry their crosses with the help and support of our love.

When the day comes that no person on earth will have to suffer alone, when every single person who is in grief, loneliness, or pain finds others pouring out the comfort and support of their surrounding love, then the salvation Jesus came to give will not seem such a scandal. It will then be experienced as the wisdom and power of God.

(This sermon has also been published in a monograph for the Sacred Heart League.)

HEAL ME

Frank L. McRae

$\mathcal{F}$aith healing is not my favorite sermon subject. Maybe my lack of personal experience conditions my interest. Possibly my understanding of healing is too restricted. I often get confused, even angry, at some claims made in the name of divine healing. But should I allow my limitations to retard other people's capacity to grow in acceptance of what is possible?

If my definition of healing is too narrowly driven, I may miss the incredible truth of God's action through many lives. The "faith factor" compels me to cry out, "Heal me," but my conditioned skepticism holds me back. Maybe new experiments in spiritual speculation will open windows of fresh understanding about healing to each of us.

I am not a scientist. I cannot weigh the possibilities of healing through faith, but I am a Christian believer. This I rely upon as I am challenged by the power of God to heal.

Like many of you, I have pondered the Biblical accounts of recorded healing. I have almost been there in Jericho when blind Bartimaeus cried out, "Jesus, Son of David, have mercy on me" (Mark 10:47). I have felt his excitement as his vision was restored.

I was present in the dusty marketplace when a woman, sick for 12 years, reached out a hand of faith to touch the hem of his garment. I almost exploded with joy when she was healed (Matthew 9:20).

I remember the same day when Jairus rushed to Jesus at the seashore. His little daughter was at the point of death. He begged for Jesus' help. Across town Jesus walked to command the child to "get up." She did. She was alive. She was healed (Luke 8:40-42, 49-55).

All my life I have lived with these ancient accounts of miraculous healing. Their truth excites and bewilders me. What really happened? What is this healing? Is God at work in other ways as well?

If God acted in ancient times to heal, can healing still happen? What is meant by healing? Maybe there is more to healing than the signs and sounds of miracles. Maybe healing is a natural experience rather than a magic trick.

We experience life from a comprehension of its dual nature. We separate the spiritual from the physical. But why? Do we believe that this division gives us greater freedom to identify and excuse our human actions? Do we label the spiritual as something special only to provide goals for living? I wonder.

If we are created by God and for God, why do we require such separation? Do we defend our sin by developing dual systems?

I believe we are created for oneness. We may choose to separate our being into spiritual, physical, physiological, social, and psychological components, but we are formed as one unit. I am increasingly convinced that healing is a process aimed at wholeness. Real healing brings into unity the varying points of our makeup. The interrelatedness of our described differences validates the claim. Our physical nature is profoundly influenced by our psychological self-perceptions. Fear releases switches in our protective physical capacities.

Healing brings into harmony those various forces at work in each of us. Healing by its very definition is a uniting factor. We refer with envy to those persons who "have it all together."

Do not Biblical lessons imply the wholeness of those who are healed? Bartimaeus called out in faith for healing. His sight was restored. He "had it all together." He was consistent with his Godly creation.

Such assumptions force us to accept the necessity of living in tune with God, our Creator. We are quick to claim our divine relationship when we are in crisis. "Our Father" may suddenly become father in deed. In suffering we cry out for God to come and arrest us from our trauma and make us whole and happy again. From hospital corridors and sickbeds, we affirm our wholeness with God.

Such pleadings are as natural as they are appropriate. They may reflect our desperation and our faith, but they erupt from deep inside ourselves.

God is not an errand boy who does favors for all who have a temporary need. Wholeness results from believing and sharing. We have much to learn about God's actions in the human situation.

Religious studies are crucial to a continuing and growing relationship with God. The record of God's action in the past may provide a prelude to present day performance. To be absorbed by religious teachings seems essential to understanding what may be God's movements today. Jesus' restoration of wholeness is the story of his public ministry.

Our unsuccessful attempts at wholeness may discourage our growth, but the challenge is to continue trying. When we abandon our faith, we are without hope.

The petition to "heal me" is a faith response to a learned understanding of God's action. At best, it summons us to a wholeness of life that is consistent with our creation. It identifies us as needy children begging for help from a loving parent.

FRANK L. McRAE

What then shall we say to this hope for healing? We recognize our limited understanding of God's action, but we have the record of God at work in history. As we progress towards wholeness with God, we become the beneficiaries of God's healing power.

In our growth we shall continue to cry out for healing, "I believe; help thou mine unbelief" (Mark 9:24).

EQUIPPED TO LIFT

Text: Luke 12:10–13   Fred C. Lofton

*D*o you have a special gift or talent? Has genetics blessed you with a rare talent, or has God equipped you with unusual abilities or aptitudes?

While you have been sick, you've had time to think about a number of things that seldom or never crossed your mind before. This is one of the positive factors that illness may bring; you can mentally look backward and forward in calm and quiet, and reminisce over the ups and downs of the past. Perhaps you've counted your blessings, and among them might be a special gift or blessing from God that has brought happiness to yourself and to others.

Just as our Heavenly Father has endowed some of us with special talents and gifts of grace, in His divine wisdom, He equipped His Son Jesus with extraordinary powers to preach, to teach, and to heal. In all of these areas of ministry, Jesus was divinely equipped to lift the bodies, minds, hearts, and souls of the people He encountered on His way to Calvary.

A healing incident in Luke's gospel is an excellent example of Jesus' God-given gift to lift. In Chapter 13:10–13, we read:

He [Jesus] was teaching in one of the synagogues on the Sabbath. And behold, there was a woman which had a spirit of infirmity eighteen years, and was bowed together, and could in no wise lift up herself. And when Jesus saw her, he called her to him, and said unto her, "Woman, thou art loosed from thine infirmity." And he laid his hands on her: and immediately she was made straight, and glorified God.

Try to visualize and internalize the scene here. See the woman before and after her wonderful encounter with the Master Healer on this most memorable day in her life. Watch Jesus teaching in the synagogue. It is the Sabbath, a day when every move He makes is closely scrutinized by the critical power brokers and politicians of that day and time. Watch Jesus as he makes eye contact with this Jewish woman, this daughter of Abraham whom Satan had bound for many miserable years. Scriptures tell us that for 18 years, she had been handicapped with a deformity that rendered her unable to lift herself up. Remember Quasimodo, the lonely outcast hunchback of Notre Dame in Victor Hugo's novel? I can imagine that the woman in this story had a physical and psychological kinship with him. I can imagine that for almost two decades she had been the victim of stares, rejection, and ridicule because she was different. Such "different people," then and now, are not always socially or intellectually accepted. Despite the advice of decision-makers in etiquette and ethics today, we still demean and ostracize those among us who are physically, mentally, or emotionally different from the way we think they ought to be.

But this bent and broken woman caught the eye and captured the compassionate nature of Jesus as He taught there in the synagogue. Isn't it amazing how Jesus could look through a crowd and spot someone who, like this poor woman, desperately needed His healing touch?

The same was true on another day in another setting. This time, Jesus was in Jerusalem, beside a pool in the sheep market where a great multitude of impotent folk lay, eagerly awaiting the time when they could step in the water and be healed. Again, Jesus penetrated the crowd, and His all-seeing eye fell on a certain physically handicapped man who had waited patiently and persistently to step into the magic pool.

> When Jesus saw him lie, and knew that he had been now a long time in that case, he saith unto him, "Wilt thou be made whole?" The impotent man answered him, "Sir, I have no man, when the water is troubled, to put me into the pool: but while I am coming, another steppeth down before me." Jesus saith unto him, "Rise, take up thy bed, and walk." And immediately, the man was made whole, and took up his bed, and walked (John 5:6–9).

But, on the other hand, we need not wait for Jesus to voluntarily and spontaneously point us out or come to us to minister to our needs. We can always bring our problems to Him and lay them at His feet. This is how the leper in Matthew 8:2, 3 did it, "Behold, there came a leper and worshipped him, saying 'Lord, if thou wilt, thou canst make me clean.' And Jesus put forth his hand, and touched him, saying, 'I will; be thou clean.' And immediately his leprosy was cleansed."

Women often sought Him too, and with His holy hands He healed them. "A woman having an issue of blood 12 years, which had spent all her living upon physicians, neither could be healed of any, came behind him and touched the border of his garment: and immediately her issue of blood stanched" (Luke 8:43, 44).

And how can one forget the beggar, blind Bartimaeus, and his poignant plea:

They came to Jericho. And as He went out of Jericho with His disciples and a great number of people, blind Bartimaeus ... sat by the highway side begging. And when he heard that it was Jesus of Nazareth, he began to cry out, and say, "Jesus, thou Son of David, have mercy on me ...." Jesus answered and said unto him, "What wilt thou that I should do unto thee?" The blind man said unto him, "Lord, that I might receive my sight." And Jesus said unto him, "Go thy way; Thy faith hath made thee whole." And immediately he received his sight and followed Jesus in the way. (Mark 10:46, 47 and 51,52)

There are many other examples of those who came to Jesus of their own volition, people whose faith in Jesus' healing power prompted them to step out with confidence and courage. Today, right now, won't you respond to the appeal of the hymnist who wrote:

Come to Jesus, come to Jesus.
Come to Jesus, just now, just now!
Come to Jesus, come to Jesus just now.

He will hear you, He will hear you,
He will hear you just now, just now!
He will hear you, He will hear you just now.

(#182 The New National Baptist Hymnal)

Not only will He hear you, but He will also heal you just now. But it is important that you sincerely believe. **You must believe** that God's Son Jesus will minister to your needs. Note that Matthew 13:58 says, "He did not many mighty works (in his own country) because of their unbelief."

Let us now return to the bowed and broken woman at the beginning of our message. Hear Jesus call her forward. See her bowed and bent body approach the heavenly Healer. Listen to His profound and liberating proclamations, "Woman, you are free from your infirmity!" See Him lay His holy hands on her body. Watch the crook in her spine relax and straighten up. "Woman, now you can stand straight and tall. Your days of counting cobblestones are over! Now you can look up and count stars. For the first time in 18 years, **you are free**!"

Hear the healed and happy woman glorifying and praising God like the slaves of old on Emancipation Day. She could now sing:

I'm so glad, Jesus lifted me!
I'm so glad, Jesus lifted me!
I'm so glad, Jesus lifted me!
I'm singing Glory Hallelujah!
Jesus lifted me!

What a dramatic moment in the life of this woman who had experienced the healing power of Jesus, together with the Holy Spirit! Share the woman's joy over the Savior who was and is equipped to lift. Join in praising the Master Healer who can lift you too.

A committed child of God believes the commands of Jesus in Matthew 7:7, "Ask, and it shall be given you; seek, and ye shall find; knock, and it shall be opened unto you." If deep in your heart you sincerely believe that this can happen in your life, pray now that God will give you whatever you ask, will heal you and restore you to good health as He did on that Sabbath day in the Jewish synagogue long ago. Believe that He can do the same thing for you today, here in Memphis, Tennessee. Say, like Jeremiah, "Heal me, O Lord, and I shall be healed ... for thou are my praise" (17:14).

Because the power of God was within His son Jesus, nothing

could stop the healing process then and nothing can stop it now!
There is healing power in His healing word and in His healing
touch today — Pentecostal power, purifying power, peace-pro-
moting power!

Now after He lifts you, what will you do? How will you
respond? When you've been lifted, you ought not be ashamed to
praise the Man who is Equipped to Lift! Sing His praises! Shout
with Joy! Say with David:

> I will sing of thy might;
> I will sing aloud of thy steadfast love in the morning.
> For thou hast been to me a fortress and a refuge in the
> day of my distress.
> O my Strength, I will sing praises to thee,
> For thou, O God, art my fortress,
> The God that shows me steadfast love.
> (Psalms 59:16,17)

SUDDEN REVERSALS

Text: Psalm 13   V. Stephen Parrish

*J*ohn was an angry young boy, hurting in ways that were never clear to me, perhaps never even clear to him. His every word and deed screamed out for attention and love, yet ironically the very things he said and did seemed to drive people farther and farther from him.

John couldn't have been more than eight years old at the time, because I was eight and we had been put in the same age group at the summer church camp. From day one he insisted on breaking the rules. During small group time he talked when the teacher was trying to talk. At evening vespers he threw the little, round pebbles that were on the ground beneath our benches. He ran in the "mess hall" when he should have been eating. During free time on Wednesday, he punched another boy in the stomach — and worse, blamed it on me! The best efforts of the counselors, first to love him and then later to rehabilitate or discipline John, met with failure. By midweek I was convinced that there was not a single religious bone in his body.

The ultimate act of apostasy, however, came early one morning during our small group time. We were all seated on a rough wooden bench in an outdoor pavilion. While the teacher was trying to lead a discussion, John took his small, black leather Bible and buried it in the pavilion's dust floor. I was shocked — and also afraid! Much of what I had heard from preachers up to that time in my life had focused upon the stern, demanding character of God. God should not be provoked because the Righteous One was quick to take action against sinners. There was no room in the life of faith for angry and pained outbursts — even from eight-year-old boys. So I was absolutely certain that God would exercise judgment on John with a bolt of lightning, a tornado, or some other instrument of divine punishment, and I wanted to be nowhere around when it happened.

I waited nervously for the end of the session and when it finally came, I got away from John and avoided him as much as I could for the rest of the week.

Despite John's reckless deed and outrageous behavior, the rest of the week went by without any natural disaster — no earthquake; no gale force wind; not even a cloudy day — as far as I can remember. What I do remember, however, was Friday evening. Everybody at camp sat around the bonfire, where songs were sung and prayers were prayed. On the other side of the circle I could see John. Although it was dark and the flickering fire caused shadows to dance across his face, I could see him clearly enough to tell that he was singing along with everyone else: "Kum ba Yah," "Spirit of the Living God," "There Is a Balm in Gilead." Shouts of anger and pain seemed to have been transformed miraculously into songs of praise.

I began to think that maybe I had been wrong about John. Maybe there was more religion to him than I had thought. I never got a chance to talk to him after the group broke up that evening, but I like to think that something happened to John between the time he arrived on Sunday afternoon and Friday evening when he sat with everyone else around the bonfire. I like to think that sometime between talking out of turn, throwing pebbles, running in the mess hall, punching other kids in the

stomach, and burying his Bible, that John had found that balm
in Gilead, had experienced some kind of healing. I like to think
that rather than raining fire and brimstone down on John
because of his anger, God accepted his anger as tormented
prayer and sent gracious showers of compassion that awakened
a new vitality in his young life. But this is much more than mere
wishful thinking on my part, because the Bible gives every reason to believe that is exactly what happened.

The honesty of Psalm 13 is startling if we take its language
seriously. The psalmist begins with five audacious questions
aimed squarely at God:

> How long, O Lord?
> Will you forget me forever?
> How long will you hide your face from me?
> How long must I bear pain in my soul,
> And have sorrow in my heart all day long?
> How long shall my enemy be exalted over me?

There is no way of knowing precisely what ailed the ancient
poet, but it is clear from the language of the psalm that the pain
was surely real. It was the kind of pain that would not let the
psalmist hide behind flattering words of false piety. Born from
the anguish of suffering, the bold outburst of the psalmist cuts
straight to the heart of the matter and lays the blame squarely on
God: "How long, O Lord? Will you forget me forever? How
long will you hide your face from me?" The poet knows that it is
fully within God's power to do something about the reality of
pain and suffering, yet God has not acted. Adding insult to
injury, the poet's enemies revel in the pain of this suffering one.

Loosened by agony's anguish, the poet's tongue takes an
even more audacious tack in verse three. "Consider, answer me,
give light," insists the psalmist. No "please" or "will you."
Instead, these are all imperatives — commands! It's the same
tone of voice that used to get me into trouble with my parents

when I was a little boy. "Buy me that toy tractor!" I demanded one Friday evening in the five and dime.

"How dare you use that tone of voice on me, young man!" my mother replied, right there in front of all the other kids. "You know better than that!" Surely the psalmist should know better than to speak to God in such a manner, but again the poet reserves sweet and flattering language for better days, and here has the outrageous grit to demand that God respond to anguished cries!

However, for all of this, perhaps the most outrageous thing about Psalm 13 is that God hears and acts, neither vengefully nor to silence the psalmist. As in the case of eight-year-old John, no thunderbolts flashed from heaven, no fire and brimstone. Instead, God acts compassionately. "I will sing to the Lord, because he has dealt bountifully with me," chants the poet. From "Answer me!" to "I will sing!" From honest lament to exuberant praise, Psalm 13 invites all of life's anguished souls to an open and honest exchange with God.

Healing can mean different things to different people. Among the meanings given for healing in the Oxford English Dictionary are these: "mending, reparation; restoration of wholeness, well-being, safety, or prosperity." Likely these are the meanings that leap to mind when we think of what it means to be healed. Miss Katie's healing was of this sort.

Miss Katie was regarded as a saint in the rural community where I pastored after I graduated from seminary. Her husband led singing, and she taught Sunday School in the small country church. She was always the first to visit the sick in the neighborhood, to take them a hot meal when they were too weak to cook, even to clean the house until they recovered. It's little wonder that the community was shocked when folks discovered that cancer had invaded Miss Katie's aging body. People were quick to return her acts of charity while she endured the nausea, the weakness, and the loss of her hair that came from the treatments she took. Initial lab reports had been grim indeed, and not much hope had been given for Miss Katie's recovery. Still, prayers were prayed by hundreds of people, and not a day passed without calls and visits. One spring day, after what had seemed an eternity of treatment and anxious waiting, more tests were run. Amazingly, miraculously most said, absolutely no signs of cancer were found! "Consider and answer me, O Lord my God! ... I will sing to the Lord, because he has dealt bountifully with me."

But the Oxford English Dictionary speaks of another kind of healing. Alongside of mending and reparation, it lists also "spiritual restoration, salvation." No less saintly than Miss Katie, Helen spent her final days in the hospital a healed woman. She was an elder in the Presbyterian church where she belonged. She was a pillar of the church in every way one might name: choir member, church school teacher, president of the Presbyterian Women, clerk of the church session. During the final days of her struggle with cancer, Helen discovered in a new way that life is somehow much larger than the earthen vessel of her weakened body. Shouts of anger, questions of doubt, and the complacency of resignation gave way to new-=found trust and confidence. "Consider and answer me, O Lord my God! ... I will sing to the Lord, because he has dealt bountifully with me."

We have no way of knowing what type of restoration the psalmist experienced. Perhaps, some have suggested, the exuberant statement of trust that closes the psalm expresses the poet's praise after being rescued from physical harm — the kind of praise that rose from Miss Katie's lips. That is surely possible. But perhaps the strong note of praise that closes the psalm was sounded in the darkest moments of physical agony. Sometimes the most compelling affirmations of faith arise from the very bowels of anguish. Genuine healing is not always synonymous with being cured from a disease. Healing comes from being able to question God with no inhibitions, understanding all the while that there is no one else who knows our pain as well as the God who suffered on the cross, or who suffered at Auschwitz, or who suffers with us. Healing comes from the conviction that we may scream at God, and finally rejoice that, cured or not, God has heard us and accepted us for who we are.

I don't know what manner of healing John experienced 33 years ago. Maybe the difference in his behavior between Sunday afternoon and Friday evening was to be explained by a letter he got that week, telling him that differences between his Mom and Dad had been resolved; or a phone call that let him know his older sister really didn't hate his insides like she had said after he slipped the spider into her purse just before leaving home Sunday afternoon. Maybe all of his problems had been worked out in his absence. That would indeed be reason to sing. Or then again, maybe John knew that he would leave camp the next morning only to return to the same intolerable family that one moment ignored him and the next ridiculed him. Perhaps he knew that the pain he had left would be waiting for him back home the moment he stepped out of the car. But somehow, in the honest expression of his anger and pain, he found that balm in Gilead only God could provide, the healing that comes from baring one's soul to God.

We'll never know for sure what happened in his life between Sunday and Friday that changed lament into praise. But of this we may be certain: when John left camp on Saturday morning, when Miss Katie left the hospital, and when Helen passed from this life into life anew, they were each embraced by the compassionate grace of God, who loves us and welcomes us just as we are.

"Consider me and answer me, O Lord my God! ... I will sing to the Lord, because he has dealt bountifully with me." May God give us the courage to be honest with ourselves and above all to be honest before and trust in the sovereignty of God's abundant grace. For surely the essence of healing, of sudden reversals, lies precisely in such honesty and trust.

YOU CAN BE BETTER THAN YOU ARE

William H. Graves

From the pen of Horatio Bonar come these words:

I dare not choose my lot;
I would not if I might;
Choose Thou for me, my God,
So shall I walk aright.
The Kingdom that I seek
Is Thine; so let the way
That leads to it be Thine,
Else, surely, I might stray.
Take Thou my cup, and it
With joy or sorrow fill;
As best to Thee may seem,
Choose Thou my good and ill.
Choose Thou for me my friends,
My sickness or my health;
Choose Thou my cares for me,
My poverty or wealth.
Not mine – not mine the choice,
In things or great or small;
Be Thou my Guide, my Strength,
My Wisdom and my All!

Many of us, it would seem, tend to order our lives by superstition. Such is the case with sickness and disease. There was a time when it was believed that sickness was the result of some hideous sin, that affliction was the result of some past misdeeds, that a child born with an impediment was the result of some mistake.

Well, the truth of the matter is that some illnesses are due to sin. In many instances, Jesus addressed the affliction of a person, telling that one to go and sin no more, or, as Jesus said to the man stricken with palsy in Mark 2:5, "Son, thy sins be forgiven thee." And we are all too familiar with the experience of Job and his friends, who accused Job of coming under the results of some dark deed.

This superstition is also evident in the minds of the disciples who queried Jesus about the man born blind when they asked the question, "Master, who committed the sin, this man, or his parents that caused his blindness" (John 9:2)?

This kind of attitude and charge is unreasonable and unkind. Jesus dispelled that notion when he said about the blind man, "Neither did this man sin, nor his parents, that he should be born blind."

I have discovered that a stay in the hospital can be a re-creating experience. I have encouraged some patients to read more, to try and develop a better relationship with the God who created us, to enlarge the spiritual vision to see goodness and discipline in sickness.

In Psalm 46, the writer affirms: "God is our refuge and strength, a very present help in trouble ... Be still and know that I am God."

David A. Ray, in his book, Where are You, God?, gives what he calls "Thought Conditioners for When You're Sick." He offers these eight suggestions:

> 1. Memorize the three principles for healthier living: a) Health is holy, and sickness is normal for God's children. b) You can participate or be helped to participate in techniques by which you can become a happier person, even when you're sick, by applying creative methods in mind and spirit. c) Many of your sicknesses can be prevented and the severity of others enormously reduced.
>
> 2. A permanent cure for sickness demands more than pills.

3. What you think affects your physical health.

4. Peace of mind is the greatest physician you can have.

5. Spiritual self-management will give a boost to your better health. (This marshals your time and energies for effective living.)

6. There is unusual therapeutic value to spiritual commitment of yourself to the Lord. (This puts your soul in focus with your maker.)

7. Add life commitment to spiritual self-management and spiritual commitment and your victory can be full. (This is to live with the facts of life and live through the challenges of life by God's power.)

8. The product is a take-charge person, and that is a healthy level of life on which to be.

Don't be afraid of your sickness, and do not let your infirmity defeat you. God said to the apostle Paul and He says to you, "My grace is sufficient for you, for my strength is made perfect in weakness" (II Corinthians 12:9).

If you know the Lord, then you can attest to the truth in this hymn:

> What a friend we have in Jesus,
> All our sins and griefs to bear!
> What a privilege to carry
> Everything to God in prayer!
> O, what peace we often forfeit,
> O, what needless pain we bear,
> All because we do not carry
> Everything to God in prayer.

And now, the Lord bless you and keep you. The Lord make His face to shine upon you and be gracious unto you. The Lord lift up the light of His countenance upon you and give you peace, both now and evermore.

GREATER WORKS THAN JESUS:
FAITH AND HEALING

Text: John 14:12–14   C. Roy Stauffer

I.

*V*ery few things are as frequently a topic of conversation and concern in our society today as is our physical health. We talk about it constantly — in public and in private. We diet. We exercise. We count our fat grams ... which has led to a booming business in "fat free" foods today. It never ceases to amaze and entertain me how people no sooner get finished with a big meal than they start talking about losing weight and dieting. There's no telling how many billions of dollars are spent annually trying to preserve our health and prolong life. But how often do we stop to think about how our religious faith might have a major influence on our mental and physical health?

Is it not true that when it comes to physical illness we usually think of doctors, drugs, hospitals, and surgery if necessary? And when it comes to mental health or mental illness do we not usually think of psychologists, psychiatrists, counselors, and mental hospitals or institutions if necessary? And when it comes to the soul and spiritual health do we not usually think of ministers, priests, rabbis, churches, religious counselors, the Bible, and religious faith? But do we not realize that these three areas of one's being — mental, physical, and spiritual ... or, body, mind and soul — are all totally interrelated? To be whole and healthy means that all three must be in good shape. Often, a mental or spiritual disorder can lead to physical problems. And a spiritual or physical disorder can lead to mental illness. And certainly physical troubles can lead to spiritual problems like depression, despair, and even feelings of futility. Dr. Carl Jung, for example, one of the most famous psychologists of our time, once said that he had never seen a patient over 35 years of age whose psychological problem didn't stem from a lack of religious outlook in life. Furthermore, he said, none of them was healed who did not regain a religious outlook (<u>Modern Man in Search of a Soul</u>). Many physicians will tell you that a high percentage of their patients are really suffering — not from physical problems — but from mental or spiritual problems. And that's why doctors often prescribe what are called "placebos" for pills that really have no medicine in them, but are given for their psychological or spiritual effect.

II.

When it comes to this subject of "faith and health" or "faith and healing," I wonder what comes to your mind. Is it a mental picture of Oral Roberts and some of his famous TV healing services of decades past or maybe some of the known frauds in the faith healing practice ... like the one know as "Marjoe"? Do you think, perhaps, of Jesus walking the dusty roads of Palestine healing the blind, the lame, the deaf, the lepers, and even raising the dead? Or maybe you think of a minister today praying in a hospital room with a person getting ready to have surgery. ... Or a family gathered in a small prayer chapel fervently praying for a loved one not to die. ... Or maybe you think of the Biblical example of anointing with oil when you pray for the sick. ... Or an ecumenical, interfaith healing service in which "hands are laid" on persons suffering from AIDS.

I have a minister friend who, several years ago, was told by a doctor that he had lung cancer. This was on a Friday, and they wanted to do surgery on Monday. Over the weekend this minister began getting his "affairs in order" thinking that this was the "beginning of the end." But also over the weekend, members of his family and his church prayed fervently for his healing. Even some elders from the church came to his room and anointed him with oils as they prayed for him. That Monday morning, before surgery, they took some more x-rays so the doctor could be sure of what he was doing. It was then that they discovered that there was not a trace of any cancer in either lung. A miracle? Do you believe in prayer and miracles? I guarantee you that my minister friend does!

There is no question about the direct relationship between one's faith in God and physical, mental and emotional healing. Faith always plays an important role in healing ... especially when both the patient and the doctor have faith. Faith realizes that God is not only the Creator of the universe, but also the Sustainer of that which He has created. Faith not only believes in the existence of God, but also that God is present and actively working in the world. Of course, God usually works through natural means, through the natural laws of the universe He created. But sometimes God can and does work through supernatural means, through intervening in the laws He has established. In both ways — both natural and supernatural — faith plays an important role in the process of healing.

One doctor observed that throughout his practice of medicine, he had noticed again and again that people with a simple trust in Jesus Christ had an attitude of quietness and peace that contributed greatly to their physical welfare ... and when surgery was required, this simple trust seemed to greatly hasten their recovery (Faith Healing by Claude A. Frazier, MD Thomas Nelson, Inc., 1973, p.8). As a minister I know from personal observations how one's faith has a direct effect on one's attitude ... and that attitude plays a major role in how well one does when facing physical problems. Especially I have seen this when people go through chemotherapy. That doctor went on to say, "I have seen cases where God had directly intervened in the healing of disease, where hopeless cases have been cured when everything else that could possibly be done had failed" (Ibid). Such experiences certainly make us realize how little we know and understand about the sovereign power and grace of God.

Something even more curious is the fact that sometimes when researchers asked both ministers and physicians what they thought of the power of prayer in healing a person's illness. In many cases it seemed the physicians had a stronger conviction about the role of faith in healing than did some ministers.

III.

Anyone skeptical of the relationship between faith and healing would certainly have a hard time reading the Gospel of Jesus Christ as found in the Bible. A typical example of this would be Mark's gospel, Chapter 1, beginning with verse 30,

Now Peter's mother-in-law lay sick with fever and immediately they told Jesus about her. And Jesus came and took her by the hand and lifted her up and the fever left her. ... That evening, at sundown, they brought to Jesus all who were sick or possessed with demons ... and He healed many who were sick with various diseases and cast out many demons.

Then skipping down to verse 40: "And a leper came to Jesus beseeching him, and kneeling said to him, 'If you will, you can make me clean.' Moved with compassion, Jesus stretched out his hand and touched him, and said to him, 'I will; be clean.' And immediately the leprosy left him, and he was made clean."

When we study all the gospel accounts like this of the healing of Jesus, we find that Jesus healed more conditions of mental illness — generally described in the New Testament as "demon-possessed" — than He did physical illness. Still, we find clear accounts of where Jesus healed epilepsy, leprosy, blindness, dumbness, lameness, paralysis, hemorrhaging, fever, and even "raised the dead." As Morton Kelsey observes in his excellent book <u>Healing and Christianity</u> (Harper & Row, 1973, p. 75): "We have no accounts of his healing headaches, backaches, stomach trouble, or muscular tension, although he undoubtedly must have, since these problems respond quite readily to suggestion and religious healing."

It's interesting how Jesus not only healed Himself, but frequently left the impression that His followers ought to be healers too. For example, in Matthew 10:7 we hear Jesus saying, "The Kingdom of Heaven is upon you. Heal the sick, raise the dead, cleanse the lepers, and cast out demons." We read how the early Church and early Christians possessed miraculous powers including the power to heal. Paul speaks of the spiritual gift of healing in I Corinthians 12, and we read of healing done by the early disciples including Peter, Ananias, and Paul. But one thing to notice in almost all the Biblical accounts of healing is the role of one's faith in being healed. Jesus said repeatedly, "Your faith has made you whole."

IV.

There is no doubt that the gifts of healing existed in the early Church. The Church, no doubt, inherited its healing tradition from its Jewish background. When a Jew was ill, it was to the rabbi he went rather than to the doctor. And the rabbi would anoint the person with oil, the best medicine of all, and then pray over him.

In the New Testament Letter of James to the early Church there is a clear instruction that if a person is ill, the leaders will anoint him with oils and pray over him. In James 5:14, 15 we read: "Is anyone among you sick? Let him call for the elders of the church, and let them pray over him, anointing with oil in the name of the Lord; and the prayer of faith will save the sick man, and the Lord will raise him up." Down through the ages the ministry of healing has been an important part of the role of the Church. In fact, many may not realize that in the Roman Catholic Church, the sacrament of extreme unction, or anointing ... or what is commonly called "the last rites" ... was originally intended as a means of a cure, not as a preparation for death as it has in the past been in the Catholic Church. The Church has always cared for the sick and had the gift of healing, except maybe for the 20th century when, for whatever reason, healing has been de-emphasized, or maybe even criticized.

But today it is all changing. Today there is a revival in the Church of the ministry of healing. Today there is a renewed emphasis on the important relationship between faith and healing, as witnessed for example in more healing services in many churches, more emphasis on prayer for the sick, in more experiences of the "laying on of hands" for the sick and anointing with oil. We also see this revived interest in the ministry of healing in such programs as the Stephen Ministry that we are now starting here at Lindenwood, and in the growing nationwide "Healing Wings" ministry, through which we have been able to sponsor little Erick Gonzales for lifesaving heart surgery this week. We see it in the fact that many churches are adding to their staff a "church nurse" to care for the health of their members. And here in Memphis, as in some other major cities in the nation, we see the Church's renewed emphasis on the ministry of healing through the establishment of such things as the Church Health Center. The specific stated mission of the Church Health Center is to "reclaim the biblical and historical commitment of the

Church to care for the poor. ... to provide affordable, quality primary health care for the working poor, children, the elderly and the homeless." It is a significant factor that the Executive Director of the Church Health Center — Dr. Scott Morris — is both a licensed physician (M.D.) and an ordained minister, a living example of witnessing to the link between faith and healing.

This renewed emphasis on faith and healing today, and note I didn't say "faith healing" but "faith and healing," is not to emphasize prayer and faith to the exclusion of scientific methods and the use of drugs and medicines. No, but it points to the fact that increasingly the relationship between prayer and healing, faith and medicine is being recognized. And the focus on healing is not just to deal with people once they become sick, but also to practice preventive medicine, to educate people and reduce the factors that lead to illness, to encourage healthy lifestyles and disease prevention. Therefore, in the church's ministry of healing today, quit-smoking programs, substance-abuse programs, nutritional information, exercise programs, AA Groups, education to avoid AIDS and other sexually transmitted diseases, and all kinds of support groups are just as important as ministering to those who are already sick. Almost one half of the deaths in this country every year are caused by tobacco, overeating and poor diet, and alcohol abuse. Think what a difference it would make if the hundreds of churches in every major city took this seriously, and worked to do something about it.

And this brings me to the main Biblical/theological observation I want to make today. When Jesus carried out His ministry of healing here on earth almost 2,000 years ago — healing the blind, the lame, the paralyzed, lepers, casting out demons, and raising the dead — He made a most interesting statement, as we read in Mark's gospel this morning. He said, "Truly, truly I say to you, he who believes in me will also do the works that I do; and ... (and here comes the key line) ... greater works than these will he do, because I go to the Father" (John 14:12).

What exactly did Jesus mean by this promise "greater works than I do will you do"?

As I have already pointed out, the early church had the same power of healing that Jesus had. But even though they could do the same things Jesus did, they didn't do greater things. Today, however, with the miracles of modern medicine, "wonder" drugs, and new technology, doctors have the power to heal and cure and operate in ways that would have seemed truly unbelievable back in Jesus' time. Can you imagine such things as a heart transplant, cornea transplant, or even modern anesthetics back then? Yes, God has given us through modern medical science the ability to do incredible things today. And, add to that the fact that when Jesus was here on earth, He could only be in one place at one time, healing one person at a time. But today, thousands of lives are saved every hour through modern medicine. When Jesus was "in the flesh," He was limited to just what He could do in Palestine. But after He died and rose again and went to the Father, He could then and now use us to do His mighty works in all places. Could this be what Jesus meant when He said, "Greater works than I do will you do because I go to the Father"?

In closing let me say that all healing comes from God. God alone is the source of all healing forces whether the healing comes through medicine, through surgery, through skilled physicians, through believing ministers, or through people like you who believe in the power of prayer. God alone is ultimately the Great Healer, the Great Physician. But God, through Christ, has made available to us today the power to do even greater works than when Jesus was here on earth.

So when you or somebody you care about is sick, do what the Scriptures tell us and pray to God. Then expect a miracle, for anything is possible with God. But as great as the joy of healing is, even greater is the power God gives us as He did Paul with his "thorn in the flesh" ... to live with it and overcome it.

"Greater works than I do will you do," said Jesus. And all of us need to claim that promise!

Prayer: O God, who art the source and power of all healing, take our brokenness and suffering and make us whole again. Open our eyes to the miracles that happen everywhere, and to the even greater miracles that can be ours ... if we just pray ... with faith. This we ask in the name of Jesus. **AMEN.**

GOD IS MORE THAN ENOUGH

Text: II Kings 4:1–7   David A. Hall

$\mathcal{T}$he Book of II Kings 4:1–7 portrays the difficult plight of a certain woman who was the widow of a deceased prophet. The scripture relates, "Now there cried a certain woman of the wives of the sons of the prophets unto Elisha, saying, 'Thy servant my husband is dead; and thou knowest that thy servant did fear the Lord; and the creditor is come to take unto him my two sons to be bondmen [slaves in a work camp].'"

The scripture from II Kings helps the reader understand the critical circumstances of this woman and how those events were closing in upon her. She was a person rendered helpless through events beyond her means of control. She was emotionally distressed, destitute, and mentally drained. The funeral of her husband was over, the mourners were gone, the sympathizers were now home and going back to their daily lives. She realized her problems were truly her own and needed solving. To this was added possible forced labor for her two sons. This woman knew she needed help quick, fast, and in a hurry. Of course, the woman had no societal or charitable relief upon which to turn for aid. Nor were there any rights to property or inheritance to fall back upon. Neither were there any social service programs in that day, and she could not expect support from the larger society, where none of the current welfare, insurance, social security, or private pension funds existed.

However, the woman did recognize that the past association her late husband shared with the prophets meant something. Her late husband was a prophet, a diligent and ardent worker for the cause of Yahweh. Certainly, the Prophet Elisha had credibility and would honor the past association. She knew there were rights derived from her late husband's peer groups that she could claim. These claims, if consistent, would obligate the leader Elisha to keep the Hebrew traditions and cause him to respond from a pure conscience to her needs. Therefore, she boldly went and addressed Elisha, the prophet.

This certain woman's name is unimportant but her story is representative of the value and worth of women in the Old Testament. She symbolized in an historic way a "class action test" for widows. In fact, the manner in which she was handled spoke directly to the prophet's integrity. More importantly, it signaled the possible fate of all prophets' widows. Exodus 21:7–11, Exodus 22:21–24 and Deuteronomy 14:28 indicate that the early Hebrews were supposed to have compassion on the helpless and the hopeless. Social justice had developed far beyond the pedestrian reactionary violence of a life for a life. To the earliest of Hebrews, social justice meant an "eye for an eye." The law in its human scope transcended the tables of stones enough to make a moral conscience known. It would have been intrinsically an immoral act for Elisha to not hear and address the woman's needs. To ignore her would be a deliberate extinguishing of all justice and hope.

The aforementioned body of scriptures created an opportunity for this woman to make a righteous appeal. Furthermore, obedience to the scripture made it possible for men to satisfy her needs. Exodus 21:7–11 was the law of Moses that prohibited abuse of females and prohibited a woman from being sold to a stranger. Women could not be dealt with "deceitfully" by an unscrupulous male. Of course, the passage deals with betrothal, but it suggests that men of moral character should be responsive to the needs of women. Exodus 22:22–24 plainly supports swift and immediate retribution upon anyone who afflicts the widow and the fatherless. Because they were usually unskilled in business and could be made destitute, one was cautioned not to cheat a defenseless woman.

Finally, Deuteronomy, Chapter 7 commanded the society to support the less fortunate during the harvest season and religious holidays. These scriptures were the basis for moral conventions and traditions that made Hebrew society more humane. This human touch would change the life of the prophet's widow.

This woman approached Elisha, a religious leader actively involved in a life and death struggle with the corrupt Royal House of Omri. Elisha's mentor, Elijah, was a battle-hardened spiritual warrior. Elijah was the just, austere and venerable prophet who trained Elisha and a college of prophets. Elijah was committed to the ouster of King Ahab and Queen Jezebel. This group of men became a formidable band and constantly did battle with the prophets of Baal. These experiences made the younger man, Elisha, resolve to obtain the blessing and inspiration of Elijah.

Elijah told the younger Elisha to follow him and upon his demise, he, Elisha, would receive the mantle of authority. Eljiah's name means "My God is Yahweh," and Elisha wanted everyone to believe he was just as powerful and capable as the old prophet. The record indicates when Elisha received the mantle of power, the prophet and the college of prophets wanted proof of his authority.

> And he took the mantle of Elijah that fell from him, and smote the waters, and said "Where is the Lord God of Elijah?" And when he also had smitten the waters, they parted hither and thither: and Elisha

went over. And when the sons of the prophets which were to view at Jericho saw him, they said, "The spirit of Elijah doth rest on Elisha." And they came to meet him, and bowed themselves to the ground before him (II Kings 2:14, 15).

With this backdrop Elisha was ushered into the role of leader upon the death of Elijah. Just as Elijah performed miracles so should Elisha. II Kings records that Elisha was equal to the task. God performed miracles for him also. Therefore, the prophet's widow came to him for help. What was her claim? She was simply a widow with two sons whose lives were in jeopardy because of their deceased father's debt. The weeping mother lamented how her husband died and that the pressure was too great upon her. People often hide behind a false sense of poor pride when confronting the difficulties of telling their pain in life. In her hour of desperation, she revealed the tyranny and possible embarrassment ahead. She explained her plight as the widow of a prophet. The prophet inquired, "What shall I do for thee? Tell me, what hast thou in the house?" The weeping woman stated because her husband died and left her with nothing, she was under great pressure to pay the creditors. She said the only thing she possessed was a pot of oil. "Thine handmaid hath not any thing in the house, save a pot of oil," said the woman.

When an individual goes to a minister or Christian and they seek healing, of course they must have it! Anyone in a hospital desires to be sent home free of his nagging illness and be empowered to face life anew. Healing is often accomplished only after one shares the pain, loneliness, and brokenness of the immediate situation with a caring individual. One can't deal with it alone, but rather, help must come and break the hold or influence of the troubles. Therefore, extreme emotional upheaval is fostered by loneliness and the solemn attitude to bear it quietly. But then, the truly appropriate thing to do is shout, "My God, come in my hour of need and sanctify this time for my deliverance." The prophet, the preacher, the Christian Worker becomes at that time a spiritual doctor. His authority transcends the vast knowledge of scientific disciplines and the certification of diplomas; he has the vision and the hope against all else. Even the impossible situation must defer to a Godly person's prayers. This is the raw stuff of faith! Here God is more than enough!

The prophet Elisha spoke with confidence and directed her to follow his orders. "Go, borrow thee vessels abroad of all thy neighbors, even empty vessels; borrow not a few. And when thou art come in, thou shalt shut the door upon thee and upon thy sons, and shalt pour out into all those vessels, and thou shalt set aside that which is full." Here was the prescription for a miraculous change in her circumstances. The orders were simply to pour oil from one vessel into another. How strange! How like God! Miracles take place because of obedience and faith merging when nothing else will work. The prophet spoke what sounded like nonsense. The hour of sanctifying had come. The prepared season of healing had started. Their orders were simply to pour oil.

This was her much needed miracle, but would it lead to her healing? Miracles take place because of obedience and faith merging when nothing else will work. The prophet spoke what sounded like utter nonsense, but if one is sick, the doctor's orders are usually followed without question. The patient is filled with trust, hope, and anticipation, that restoration to health through the doctor's care will be possible. A person in need of healing is equally anticipating being made whole through Christ. I Corinthians 12:9 indicates that God grants spiritual gifts of working healings. Healing is characterized as bringing health to the sick by means of prayer. Whereas, in verse 10, the reader is informed that miracles are different. A miracle is the result of the power of God altering nature. An example is the parting of the Red Sea. This was a miracle of great deliverance, but not healing. In the case of the woman in this message, she needed both a healing and a miracle. All healings are miracles, but not all miracles are healing.

To be healed requires a special faith of both the healer and the healed. The willingness to act in concert with belief opens the possibilities of faith and the power for healing, Hebrew 11:1 states, "Now faith is the substance of things hoped for, the evidence of things not seen." Faith breaks down the stubborn need to see and moves the hopeful to the larger reality that God offers. When God is recognized as big enough to stand between the doom and the darkness of hopelessness, the bad record of one's medical chart, etc., then the hopeful aspects of healing take over. This is stated in James 5:4, "Is any sick among you? Let him call for the elders of the church, and let them pray over him, anointing him with oil in the name of the Lord."

Therefore, with hopeful expectations the woman went home to do as the prophet instructed. How many times do we modern Christians, confronted with similar challenges that take extreme faith, fail? Without faith we are doomed to miss our blessing, because faith is the essential element to ensure success. If the borders of reason appear to be high walls of frustration, then the only answer seen on the horizon is faith. Alas, she realized that the prophet's words were her best hope. She really didn't understand what he was asking her to do. She simply went for it.

First, she ordered her boys to go gather the vessels. When challenged to have faith one must merely trust God, which is hard to do, not because God has failed, but because we are found lacking. Maybe she realized that if her sons failed to participate, they would only register complaints and be idle when needed most. Second, after they collected the pots (vessels), she assembled them all around the house and shut the door. One of the greatest challenges to faith is interference or the misinterpretation of events by those who stand on the peripher, and leer into our situations. From the periphery people normally speak — quickly, frankly, and loudly — about another person's concerns, disappointments and proclaim what they would do under the same circumstances. She shut the door on all of that. Last, she poured the oil from the main pot into the others and filled every pot in the house. To her surprise the oil continued to pour and never diminished.

Now, about these events her understanding was far from perfect. Her house was filled with oil. She did not see what had happened through faith and obedience. The result was miraculous, and a wonder to behold. As stated before, miracles are not healing in every case. Her miracle was in the abundance of the oil. In her mind she was yet poor and destitute, even sick. She was yet grief-stricken and sick about her plight, and now all she had was a house filled with oil. The woman left home crying and upset because she did not understand, nor appreciate, what God had done for her. She lamented to Elisha that her house was filled with oil, but the debts were unpaid, the creditor was yet threatening to take her sons, and she was broke, helpless, and utterly an emotional wreck.

This woman needed more than a miracle; she needed healing from lack of faith and a poor understanding about God's faithfulness. "Healing comes from sharing our experiences," stated Henry Nouwen, author of The Wounded Healer. Nouwen was convinced that personal loneliness puts an individual in touch with pain and suffering. If our illness is private, no one will know the extent of our pain. Loneliness pushes an individual to share the feelings and the pains.

This loneliness has a paradoxical aspect. The loneliness pushes one to the altar of grace. As Nouwen stated, "But the more I think of loneliness, it is like the Grand Canyon — a deep incision in the surface of our existence which has become an inexhaustible source of beauty and self-understanding."

She told the prophet that she only had a house filled with oil. He informed her, "Go sell the oil, and pay thy debt, and live thou and thy children of the rest." Suddenly, she was healed because of her improved understanding of God's powers unfolding within her life.

How can one adequately end this word of faith? God is more than enough! God is more than our illness and concerns. Can anyone imagine this woman's life after she sold the oil? She probably sold out, but kept one pot, the original vessel. Imagine her placing that pot in the center of the floor where everyone could see it. Imagine her placing plants around it and maybe two chairs in front of it. Then, she sits there and waits for someone to come visit her, crying, hurt, sick, and crazy. Imagine her telling that individual to sit down. And finally, imagine her saying, "I remember when I was sick, hurt, crazy, and hopeless, but do you see that pot?" **God is more than enough!**

DEAF AND MUTE ...
THEN 'OPENED' AND HEALED!!

Text: Mark 7:31–37   Douglass M. Bailey, III

*Y*ou are deaf! For years, maybe all of your life, you have lived in the stark, silent world of "not hearing."

Oh, the world speaks to you. You watch the wind blowing through the trees, but you do not hear the rustle of the leaves. You watch the waters of the lake lap up against the shore, but you've never heard the waves. You watch people, with great frustration, trying to communicate with you, but you have never heard a human word. You live in a world where you are a prisoner of silence.

And, you have another handicap. You are mute. With minimal research, one learns that deafness is often accompanied by muteness. It is very difficult for a child to learn how to speak words if one does not hear words. Whatever the reason, you are mute. It is as though something is locked in your throat, or in your vocal cords, or in your tongue. Your voice is mute!

And, because you are deaf and mute, you are also poor. The world seems to discount persons with handicaps. When you have two handicaps, unable to hear and unable to speak, then there are no jobs for you, and you are in poverty. You are poor.

One day, communication is somehow given to you that Jesus is coming to your village. The people in the village, maybe because they are so frustrated at trying to communicate with you, maybe because they have such faith in this Jesus, the village people beg Jesus to come and lay His hands on you. And He does! You don't understand what is happening, but this is what you recall ... first, Jesus touches you. For so long you have felt "untouchable" because of your handicaps, but Jesus breaks through those barriers and touches you. He places His hands in your blocked ears. He places His fingers on your tongue and on your constricted throat. The word for "blockage" or "constriction" is the same root word for "anger" and "anxiety." So, Jesus is touching you where you are most constricted, most anxious and probably most angry.

A second thing He does is ... looking up to heaven, He sighs. Yes, as you look up and watch Him, holding Him as He is holding you, you notice that Jesus is sighing over you, that He is praying over you, crying over you. Jesus is crying over you!

Later, you hear about the word that He whispers. He uses an old Aramaic word, "Ephphatha" which means, "be opened." Ears, "be opened." Throat and tongue, "be opened." Be healed! You can't explain it. All of a sudden for the first time in your life, your ears now are opened, and you hear the sound of the wind that the hearing world takes for granted. You hear the sound of human words; you even hear the sacred sound of someone calling your name for the first time. And then, you hear your own voice speak your very first words.

Because you are Jewish and because you know your Hebrew Scripture, you recall the words in the book of the prophet Isaiah, "When God comes, the eyes of the blind will be opened and the ears of the deaf will be unstopped; and the people who are lame will leap like deer, and the people who are speechless will sing for joy" (Isaiah 35:4–7). You know, deep in your soul you know, that the Kingdom of God is breaking open, even in your own life.

I believe that hidden in this Gospel story (Mark 7:31–37) about deafness and muteness there are some essential ingredients for healing ... and for our deep reflection.

The first ingredient is the sacred power of touch. In healing, as in other matters, Jesus seeks to touch us where we hurt. Christ touches us in the place where we are most anxious, where our anger and our pain may be the greatest, where our need is the most. If you are deaf and if you are mute, Jesus places His hands in your ears, and He touches that place where you cannot speak. The Gospel story states that He takes His own saliva and places it in those locations where we are in need. That may seem strange to us, in our late 20th Century culture, but saliva in the first century is understood to be medicine. So, in this portrait, complete with saliva, I see Jesus taking our late 20th century medicine, our medical knowledge, all of the gifts of modern medical science, and joining our medical science with His healing touch. I want to lift up and support all who practice medicine, in any form, as being partners of the Great Physician in the healing ministry.

Jesus touches each of us and brings the "saliva" of modern medical science to our healing. You remember, do you not, the power of someone physically touching you when you needed to be touched. In the same way the spirit of Christ reaches out and touches us where we hurt and need it. The sacred power of touch is part of our healing.

On Thursdays, during our ecumenical healing service, after receiving the Sacrament of Eucharist, people remain at the altar rail, and each person is individually anointed with oil and prayed over (or for others) and touched with the Sacrament of Christ's presence. In that touch during a Thursday healing service, Christ is seeking to touch us where we need our deepest healing.

Secondly, He prays over us! Do you believe that? Can you and I believe that Jesus is praying over us as though we, each of us, are the only persons in the world that Jesus has time to pray for? Yes, Jesus is praying with passion and compassion about our healing.

In the Gospel story for today, it states, "He looks up to heaven and sighs." He prays by sighing. He groans because maybe He doesn't have the words. He sighs over us. He cries over us. He has compassion for our hurt and pain. The Greek word for "compassion" is "splagchnizomai," which means that it comes from Jesus' deepest feeling center: His bowels, His intestines, and His heart. Compassion is not just an action on the outside; it comes from deep in one's interior ... in the very center space of our feelings. So it is with compassion and sighing and crying that Jesus is praying for you and me in our times of illness and hurt and pain and suffering.

I have learned that some of my prayers that seem to be most useful in my own personal life are those that I can't find words for ... prayers where I just have to sigh ... prayers where I groan ... those that come from deep within my bowels because I don't know what to say. How does one pray for a Rwandan child who has lost parents and now is a refugee and fending for life at four years of age? These children are in Rwanda by the hundreds, by the thousands. How do you find words for that kind of horror? You just sigh over it. How do you find words for the 11-year-old children in our cities today with guns killing other 11-year-old children? How do you find words for people who, because of gang warfare in Memphis, are caught in cross-fire and innocently gunned down? How do you find words for that? I can't. In my prayers, I cry over my city. How do you sit by the bedside of a young woman who has cancer, and because of the massive doses of chemotherapy and radiation, is now so weakened that she can't take any more medicine because her body is a sponge that cannot absorb any more? You just sit beside her and touch her and sigh your compassion for her. In the same fashion Jesus prays for our healing.

A third ingredient for our healing is found in that word that Jesus whispers over us. "Ephphatha!" "Be opened!" Ears, "be opened." Throat, "be opened." AIDS, "be driven away." Cancer, "be healed." Over the whole of creation, Jesus, the Great Physician, is proclaiming, "Be healed. Be opened."

That is what I need to hear because to be opened is to become more expectant. I would suppose that what each of us needs is a greater sense of expectancy ... that Christ is going to do Christ's unique thing in your life and mine, which is to heal. We need to believe and to expect that Christ, the Good Doctor, will touch and pray and heal our needs, and the world's deepest needs.

Yes, I need to become more expectant. In my preparation and writing the words of this homily, I became so conscious of needing a greater sense of expectation that Christ would translate in your hearts and in your souls what you need to hear from my inadequate words. I wonder ... do you listen to these words with the spirit of expectation ... as though you are "leaning forward" to hear Christ speak to you? Maybe white congregations need to begin to act like black congregations ... to lean forward in our pews as though we are really expecting to hear the word of the Lord for us today. Did you come expecting that? Do I expect that my words can somehow become God's words? To be more expectant is to be in a position of "ephphatha," more "open" to Christ touching and healing our life.

Dr. Fred Craddock, a great homiletics professor, loves to tell stories. He tells the story, maybe poking fun at us Episcopalians, about a young Episcopal priest who, soon after ordination, goes to make hospital rounds. On his hospital list is Margaret who is very ill, old in age, maybe in her late eighties, at the point of death and probably will not leave the hospital. He goes in feeling inadequate and not knowing what to do. She is barely able to communicate, and he is uncomfortable about how to do it. Finally he says to her, "Would you like for me to have a prayer with you?"

And she says, "I sure hope you will."

He gives a "wonderful," cautious Episcopal prayer, "Lord I

wish you would send your healing Holy Spirit into the life of this, your servant, Margaret, and heal her if it is your will ... but if it is not your will, Oh Lord, if it is not your will to heal her, then give her strength and give her the assurance to live with what she must live with through the end of her days. In the name of Christ our Lord, we pray. Amen."

He looks down at Margaret. Her eyes open, and she says, "Thank you. Thank you. I feel better."

She raises up in bed, and the priest says, "Don't overdo it."

"I feel better. Thank you, young man, for that prayer. That was wonderful. I feel better. I feel like I am sort of healed." She whips her legs over the edge of the bed, and she says, "Yes, I am certain of it. I am better." The young priest wonders what is happening. He doesn't know what to do. He watches her walk out to the nurses' station where she declares, "Look, I am healed."

The young priest, greatly confused, walks to the elevator, goes down the elevator and out into the parking lot. Just as he is ready to open the car door, he looks up and says, "Don't you ever do that to me again."

We laugh about that story, but we don't live with near enough of the spirit of expectation. But, Ann and Bobby Leatherman do. The Leatherman/Orgill family lives with expectation, and here is their story.

Ann and Bobby's young baby developed a critical malignant tumor in the lining around her heart. It was strangling young Liza's heart. St. Jude Hospital had only seen three cases like this in all of its history. The doctors operated, and surgically removed as much of the tumor as they could. The prognosis was terrible for Liza. Bobby, Ann, family members, extended family, and close friends were here every Thursday at our healing service, expectant that Liza was going to be healed miraculously, when prognosis was terrible. The doctors said it couldn't get any worse. Little Liza was in a coma for significant periods of time. That did not stop Ann and family and friends. Whenever Ann couldn't be here, she would send representatives to the Healing

Service. They would all come to the altar rail and receive the anointing touch and the "sighing" prayers of the clergy and the prayers of the people. They would come expectant Thursday after Thursday after Thursday, never giving in, always expectant. Then came the word that the tumor was disappearing; then came the word that the tumor had shrunk significantly; then came the word that there was no tumor at all. Liza is a portrait out of the New Testament; she is a "miracle," like many other healing miracles you have heard and may personally know about. Weeks later, Ann came back to our healing service to tell "a mother's story of the healing of her child." It was moving for all of us … a testimony to the power of expectant prayer.

I wonder, in those times of our own severe medical distress or emotional trauma, I wonder if you can believe that the Kingdom of God, the great cosmic Christ comes to us in these moments of our need, and touches us where we hurt the most. And, can you believe that He sighs over us? He cries over us. He prays over us. Then He whispers the ancient word, "Ephphatha." Be opened. In this very hour, be healed. I wonder if you, like Isaiah of old, can believe there are times when Christ draws near and there is an opening, there is a healing. Ears that were deaf are now unstopped, and for one who had no speech, there is now glorious singing, maybe singing that great old hymn, "There's a wideness in God's mercy, like a wideness in the sea …. There is healing in his blood, (for the likes of you and me)." Thanks be to God!

In the name of God, our Creator, our Redeemer, and our Sacred Companion. **AMEN.**

EPILOGUE

Words of hope and healing are important to all people of faith. Our scriptures and our traditions are filled with both at every turn, and yet there truly remains something mysterious about each one. As a physician, I often see people who are desperate for healing but have lost all hope. When this happens to someone, it is a terrible thing to witness. How is it possible to give another person hope?

Recently, I treated a man who was extremely anxious about his health, but there did not seem to be anything physically bothering him. In an attempt to comfort him, I jokingly told him that there was one thing I was certain of and that was he was going to die eventually, but I did not think it would be anytime soon. Terribly distraught, he called back the next day and spoke to the nurse. "The doctor told me I am going to die," he said. With that belief, he had lost all hope. I had to quickly set things straight, for to take away someone's hope is an act approaching unforgivable.

The religious community has an obligation to lift up hope for healing — body and spirit — to all of God's children. These sermons show the various ways that this message is being spoken by pastors of diverse congregations throughout Memphis, Tennessee. The message is not always the same, because the fullness of God's actions and the hope and healing those actions bring is broad and deep. The message, however, expresses the many ways that religious congregations have come to experience and share the word of hope and healing in today's suffering world.

In addition to the power of the spoken word, Memphis' congregations have also put faith into action in a ministry of healing known as the Church Health Center.

Located in Midtown Memphis, the Church Health Center provides affordable health care to the working poor, elderly, children and homeless of Shelby County, Tennessee. It provides quality primary medical, dental, optometry and pastoral counseling services, along with many health education programs. In many cases, the Center also provides medicines to its uninsured patients.

The Center is open from early morning to late evening on weekdays and is open on Saturdays, so patients do not have to miss work to see the doctor. The evening and Saturday hours are staffed by volunteer doctors, nurses, dentists and optometrists. Non-professional volunteers perform many of the support services needed to operate the Center. There are also literally hundreds of specialist physicians and dentists who volunteer to see patients in their own offices free of charge. The city's hospitals, laboratories and ancillary medical facilities also generously donate services and supplies.

Funding for the Center comes from patients' fees — based on a sliding scale — and donations from individuals, churches, businesses and foundations. The Church Health Center receives no government funding through grants.

More than 18,000 patient visits occur each year, all because Memphians of faith have heard the word of hope and healing preached in their sanctuaries. This word — brimming with power and laden with comfort — is for all that hear it. It is a word that makes faith come alive and seem vibrant.

For all of us, it is true that one day we will surely die, but the final word is that there is hope that we will be healed in body and spirit, and that God will draw us close to the divine source of love. But until that day comes, there is work to be done in this broken and suffering world. You and I are called to serve God's creation in a ministry of hope and healing.

Each of us must now begin to answer that call in earnest. It is one of the most important things we will ever do.

BIOGRAPHIES

THE CONTRIBUTORS
AND THEIR CONGREGATIONS

William Allen Adkins, Jr., Pastor and Organizer
Bill Adkins is the pastor of Greater Imani Church and Christian Center. A graduate of Christian Brothers University, Pastor Adkins' ministry has led him from Memphis to Ghana, Africa, where he has helped to establish a church. He is founder and president of the Afrocentric Theology Institute.
Greater Imani Church and Christian Center
Greater Imani was organized in 1989 by Pastor Bill Adkins and 29 members. Today Greater Imani Church and Christian Center has a membership of 5,000 with a mission in Kumasi, Ghana, which recently opened a medical center. Greater Imani Church and Christian Center is located at 1000 South Cooper Street.

Douglass M. Bailey, III, M.Div., D.Min., D.D., Rector
Doug Bailey has been the rector of Calvary Episcopal

Church for 16 years. He is the founder and continuing Board member of six urban ministry non-profit corporations established by Calvary Church. He serves the National Episcopal Church as the Presiding Bishop's appointed representative for Episcopal mission work in Brazil and serves on the National Board of the Episcopal Radio and TV Foundation, Inc.

Calvary Episcopal Church

Historic Calvary Church, established in 1882, is in the heart of Downtown Memphis. Major parish emphasis has been put on congregational development, urban ministry and congregational balance between faith formation and faith in action. The church is recognized as one of the most vigorous and fastest-growing urban Episcopal Churches in America. Calvary Episcopal Church is located at 102 North Second.

William R. Bouknight, III, M.Div., D.Min., Senior Minister

Bill Bouknight is the senior minister of Christ United Methodist Church. A native of South Carolina, he was educated at Duke University, the University of Edinburgh and Yale Divinity School. In 1988, Reverend Dr. Bouknight was awarded the honorary Doctor of Divinity degree from Wofford College.

Christ United Methodist Church

With over 6,000 members, Christ United Methodist Church is one of the largest churches in Memphis. Today, it ranks as a national leader in the United Methodist denomination. The congregation's missional programs reach from the Memphis area to the former Soviet Union. Christ United Methodist Church is located at 4488 Poplar Avenue.

Lee R. Brown, M.Div., D.D., Senior Pastor

Lee Brown was called to Springdale Baptist, his first pastorate in September 1979. Pastor Brown is the Memphis Baptist Ministerial Association's immediate past president. He is a member of the Tennessee Baptist Missionary &

Educational Convention's Congress's and the National Baptist Congress of Christian Education's faculties.

Springdale Baptist Church

Springdale Baptist Church was organized in 1928 by Reverend S.L. Thompson. During Pastor Brown's tenure, the church has begun an inclusive Christian education program, a six-week Christian discipleship session, an annual church Retreat, a leadership school and a sister church in Kenya. Springdale Baptist Church is located at 1193 Springdale.

Kimberly Campbell, M.Div., Associate Minister

Kim Campbell is Associate Minister at Kingsway Christian Church (Disciples of Christ), where she has served since 1990. She holds a Bachelor of Arts degree from Southwest Texas State University and a Master of Divinity degree from Brite Divinity School (Texas Christian University).

Kingsway Christian Church

Kingsway Christian Church is an 800-member congregation affiliated with the Christian Church (Disciples of Christ). Kingsway's Schaeffer Memorial Chapel is one of the few places of worship in the city which remains open to the community 24 hours a day for prayer and meditation. The congregation also supports a pastoral counseling ministry which has served the community since 1987. Kingsway Christian Church is located at 6310 Poplar Avenue.

Burton D. Carley, Th.M., Minister

Burton Carley is a graduate of Texas Christian University and Boston University School of Theology. Before being called in 1983 to the First Unitarian Church of Memphis, he served congregations in Massachusetts and Louisiana. He is a past president of the Memphis Ministers Association.

First Unitarian Church

The First Unitarian Church of Memphis was founded in 1893 and moved to its current site on the Mississippi River bluff in 1966. The building won an architectural award and became known as the Church of the River. The church is a member of the Unitarian Universalist Association. The First Unitarian Church is located at 292 Virginia Avenue West.

James Malone Coleman, M.Div., D.Min., Bishop
Episcopal Diocese of West Tennessee

Jim Coleman was elected to be the bishop coadjutor of the Diocese of West Tennessee in June 1993. Bishop Coleman served in the United States Army before receiving his Bachelors of Science from the University of Tennessee, his Master of Divinity from the University of the South and a Doctorate of Ministry in Pastoral Theology from Wake Forest University.

Cheryl Cornish, M.Div., Pastor

Cheryl Cornish came to First Congregational Church in 1988. She received her Bachelor of Arts from Williams College and a Master of Divinity from Yale University. A native of Nebraska, Reverend. Cornish is active in the Memphis community through her participation in numerous organizations.

First Congregational Church

First Congregational United Church of Christ dates its history back to the Civil War when it was called "Strangers Church" — a church that welcomed travellers in the business district. Today, First Congregational has active partnerships with LeMoyne-Owen College, Memphis Area RAIN and the Mid-South Peace and Justice Center. First Congregational United Church of Christ is located at 234 South Watkins.

William H. Graves, M.Div., D.Min., Bishop

William Graves, the 42nd bishop of the Christian Methodist Episcopal Church, has been the presiding prelate of the First Episcopal District, comprising the states of Tennessee and Arkansas for the past 12 1/2 years. He completed his undergraduate studies at Lane College, graduate studies at Phillips

School of Theology (ITC and advanced studies), and his Doctorate of Ministry at Claremont School of Religion.

Micah D. Greenstein, M.A.H.L., M.P.A., Associate Rabbi

Micah Greenstein earned his degrees from Cornell University, Harvard University and the Hebrew Union College - Jewish Institute of Religion. He has published articles in the CCAR Journal and Religious Studies Review, and has co-authored a chapter on Black-Jewish relations for an upcoming anthology entitled Southern Rabbis and Civil Rights.

Temple Israel

Temple Israel was organized in 1853 under the name Congregation Children of Israel. It continues to be actively involved in the religious, civic and cultural life of the community-at-large, as well as to strengthen its ties with the household of Israel worldwide. Temple Israel is located at 1376 East Massey Road in East Memphis.

David A. Hall, M.Div., D.Min., Pastor

David Hall is a graduate of Butler University (Bachelor of Arts); the Interdenominational Theological Center (Master of Divinity); and the McCormick Theological Seminary (Doctorate of Ministry). Dr. Hall, serves in the C.O.G.I.C. Headquarters Jurisdiction as general secretary and director of Christian Education.

Temple Church of God In Christ

The Temple Church of God In Christ had its beginning in 1910 under the leadership of Bishop Charles Harrison Mason, founder of the Church of God In Christ. Among the congregation's ministries are its youth ministry, clothing and food relief, prison ministry, puppet ministry, day care, ministry to the fatherless and mass media efforts. The Temple Church of God In Christ is located at 672 South Lauderdale Street.

Alfred DeWayne Hill, M.Div., D.Min., Senior Pastor
Alfred Hill received a Bachelor of Arts from the American Baptist College, a Master of Divinity from Memphis Theological Seminary and a Doctoratein Ministry from Louisville Presbyterian Theological Seminary. He serves as an adjunct professor of Religion and Philosophy at LeMoyne-Owen College and is the director of the Pastor's Conference of the Tennessee Baptist Missionary and Educational Convention.

Pilgrim Rest Baptist Church
The Pilgrim Rest Church of Memphis has more than 1,000 members and has been in existence for 82 years. Its roots are deep in the African American tradition. The Church fosters a variety of ministries designed to meet the needs of the oppressed, homeless, poor and the illiterate. Pilgrim Rest Church is located at 491 East McLemore Avenue.

Benjamin Lawson Hooks, J.D., Senior Pastor
Ben Hooks, formerly the executive director of the National Association for the Advancement of Colored People (NAACP), attended LeMoyne-College and Howard University. He also received a Juris Doctorate from DePaul University College of Law. He was appointed to the FCC by President Nixon. He is the former pastor of Greater New Mount Moriah Baptist Church in Detroit.

Greater Middle Baptist Church
Greater Middle Baptist Church was organized in 1848 for freed slaves. Through Reverend Hooks' vision and leadership, Greater Middle Baptist is a dedicated mentoring and educational resource in the Memphis community. Greater Middle Baptist Church is located at 2455 Lamar Avenue.

Alvin O'Neal Jackson, M.Div., D.Min., Senior Pastor
Alvin Jackson is the senior pastor of the Mississippi

Boulevard Christian Church. Dr. Jackson received his Bachelor of Arts Degree from Butler University, a Master of Divinity Degree from Duke University School of Divinity and a Doctor of Ministry Degree from United Theological Seminary in Ohio.

Mississippi Boulevard Christian Church

Mississippi Boulevard Christian Church is the largest and fastest-growing congregation of the Christian Church (Disciples of Christ) in America. With a participating membership of over 7,000, the church is committed to attracting and winning members, developing them to Christ–like maturity, and empowering them for a meaningful ministry in the church and the world. Mississippi Boulevard Christian Church is located at 70 North Bellevue Avenue.

David M. Knight, M.A., S.T.D., Priest

David Knight speaks four languages and has a Master or Arts from Gonzaga University and a Doctorate in Theology from Catholic University of America. For the past 15 years, his focus has been on pastoral plans and programs of spiritual growth for the laity. He has published 29 books and over 50 articles, and he has given more than 400 workshops, missions and retreats on lay spirituality and on the religious vows throughout the world.

Sacred Heart Catholic Church

Sacred Heart Church is a Catholic parish in Midtown Memphis, serving approximately 1,000 families. Half of the members speak Spanish, and more than 100 are Vietnamese. The parish values its multicultural makeup and works at forming one community of different races, ethnic groups, and social and economic categories. Sacred Heart Church is located at 1324 Jefferson Avenue.

James M. Latimer, M.Div., D.D., D.L., Senior Pastor

Jimmy Latimer received his Bachelor of Arts from Bethel College and a Master of Divinity from Memphis Theological Seminary. He also received a Doctorate of Divinity from Florida Bible College and a Doctorate of Law degree from Crichton College. In 1985, Dr. Latimer wrote the introductions to the Books of Ephesians and II Thessalonians for the Christian Life Bible.

Central Church

Central Church came into being in 1896 as Central Cumberland Presbyterian Church. Central Church has since grown to more than 7,500 members. Some of Central's pioneer ministry work includes adolescent substance abuse treatment, ministry to singles, ministry to homosexuals, and ministry for adults with substance abuse, as well as a large counseling ministry. Central Church is located at 6655 Winchester Road.

Louise Upchurch Lawson, M.Div., Associate Pastor

Louise Lawson is a graduate of Duke University and Princeton Theological Seminary. She was the first ordained woman minister to serve a Memphis area church. She began her ministry in 1976 as an associate pastor at Idlewild Presbyterian Church, where she served for 15 years.

Germantown Presbyterian Church

A congregation of the Presbyterian Church (USA), Germantown Presbyterian Church was founded on March 24, 1838. During its 157 years of active ministry, Germantown Presbyterian has sought to minister in the name of Christ. Germantown Presbyterian is located at 2363 South Germantown Road.

Fred C. Lofton, M.Div., D.Min., Pastor

Fred Lofton received degrees from Morehouse College,

the University of Southern California and Emory University. He has served as the president of the Progressive National Baptist Convention and has served on numerous local and national boards.

Metropolitan Baptist Church

The Metropolitan Baptist Church was founded in 1889. It is a church which is deeply committed to the spiritual and social well-being of its church family and the community-at-large. Metropolitan Baptist Church is located at 767 Walker Avenue.

James S. Lowry, M.Div., Senior Pastor

Jim Lowry grew up in Great Falls, South Carolina. He has degrees from Presbyterian College and Columbia Theological Seminary. A minister of the Presbyterian Church (USA), he served Presbyterian churches in Alabama, Florida and South Carolina before coming in May 1992 to Idlewild Presbyterian Church.

Idlewild Presbyterian Church

Idlewild Presbyterian Church was established in early 1891 from a merger of a remnant of Park Avenue Presbyterian Church (est. 1867) and a Sunday school in the Idlewild subdivision. It is a congregation of the Presbyterian Church (USA) and is well-known for its commitment to ministry in the community. Idlewild Presbyterian Church is located at 1750 Union Avenue.

Frank Lewis McRae, M.Div., D.D., Pastor

Frank McRae, a graduate of Candler School of Theology at Emory University, has been the pastor of St. John's United Methodist Church since June 1976. His focus of ministry has been the urban poor. He is a founding board member of the Metropolitan Interfaith Association and is active in the National Conference of Christians and Jews and the Church Health Center.

St. John's United Methodist Church

St. John's United Methodist Church is one of the oldest Methodist churches in Memphis. It currently supports a wide variety of programs which include a soup kitchen, a food pantry, a senior citizens day program, as well as extensive involvement in the Church Health Center, Friends for Life and Family Link. St. John's United Methodist Church is located at 1207 Peabody Avenue.

V. Steven Parrish, M.Div., Ph.D., Associate Professor

Steven Parrish is an associate professor at Memphis Theological Seminary and holds degrees from Bethel College, Memphis Theological Seminary and Vanderbilt University. Dr. Parrish has also contributed an article on "Creation" to the <u>Mercer Dictionary of the Bible</u>. He is presently writing a book that examines creation theology in the Book of Psalms.

Memphis Theological Seminary

Memphis Theological Seminary is an educational institution of the Cumberland Presbyterian Church. The ecumenical character of the seminary is reflected by the nearly 30 denominations represented among the students and faculty. Memphis Theological Seminary is fully accredited to offer the M.A.R., the M.Div. and the Ph.D. degrees. The campus is located on 2.3 acres at 168 East Parkway South.

Brooks Ramsey, M.Div. D.Min., Co-Director
Pastoral Counseling and Consultation Center

Brooks Ramsey graduated from Union University with a Bachelor of Arts, Southwestern Baptist Theological Seminary with a Master of Divinity and Eden Theological Seminary with a Doctorate of Ministry. He is ordained in the American Baptist Church and was in pastoral ministry for 25 years. He is licensed as a marriage and family therapist, and has most recently practiced as a pastoral counselor.

Kenneth S. Robinson, M.Div., M.D. Senior Pastor

Kenneth Robinson holds a Bachelor of Arts, from Harvard University; a Doctorate of Medicine from Harvard Medical School; and a Master of Divinity from Vanderbilt Divinity School. His ministerial career, which began with his acceptance of the call to preach while in medical school, has been characterized by spiritual, numeric and programmatic community and by church growth.

St. Andrew African Methodist Episcopal Church

Founded in 1866, Saint Andrew African Methodist Episcopal Church continues to embrace holistic approaches to spiritual enrichment and has integrated programs from alcohol/drug abuse prevention and emergency food and clothing distribution, to family life enrichment and child care services, as well as academic and job skills and youth activities. Saint Andrew African Methodist Episcopal Church is located at 867 South Parkway East.

J. Peter Sartain, S.T.L., S.T.B., V.G., Priest

Peter Sartain was ordained a Catholic priest in 1978 after having completed his seminary training at the Pontifical North American College in Rome, Italy. Since ordination, he has served in several parishes in Memphis. He is currently pastor of St. Louis Parish and Vicar General of the Catholic Diocese of Memphis.

St. Louis Church

St. Louis Catholic Church was founded in 1956. A Catholic elementary school has been part of the parish since its inception. With almost 1,800 households, St. Louis is well-known for its extensive parishioner involvement in a broad range of religious and social programs. St. Louis Catholic Church is located at 5192 Shady Grove Road.

John Prentis Sartelle, Sr., M.Div., Senior Minister

For the past 17 years, John Sartelle has been the senior

minister of the Independent Presbyterian Church. He is a graduate of King College and Columbia Theological Seminary. In 1973, Reverend Sartelle was one of the founding members of The Presbyterian Church in America. He is author of the much-used booklet, "Infant Baptism: What Christian Parents Should Know."

Independent Presbyterian Church

Independent Presbyterian Church is a growing church built on the rich heritage of the Reformed Faith, with a high view of worship and a desire to follow Christ in all of life — from the executive boardrooms to the streets of the inner city. Independent Presbyterian Church is located at 4738 Walnut Grove Road.

Nancy Hastings Sehested, M.Div., Pastor

Nancy Hastings Sehested received her Master of Divinity from Union Theological Seminary in New York City. She has been featured in several television programs including Bill Moyers' special series on religion and "Sword & Spirit: A Six-Part Documentary Series Exploring the Cutting Edge of Christianity Around the World."

Prescott Memorial Baptist Church

For over 75 years, Prescott Memorial Baptist Church has understood its mission as a healing and reconciling community of Christ. With 300 members, Prescott Memorial is a small church with a large vision and a strong commitment to express the love of Christ in the world. Prescott Memorial Baptist Church is located at 499 Patterson.

Richard D. Sisk, M.Div., D.Min., Pastor

Dick Sisk holds a Bachelor of Science in Education From Texas Tech University and two master's degrees from Criswell Center for Biblical Studies and Southwestern Baptist Theological Seminary. He also received his Doctorate of Ministry degree from Southwestern Baptist

Theological Seminary, and has pastored churches throughout the world before coming to Broadmoor in 1991.

Broadmoor Baptist Church

In March 13, 1960, Broadmoor Chapel became Broadmoor Baptist Church, part of the Shelby Baptist Association, Tennessee Baptist Convention and the Southern Baptist Convention. God continues to bless: the fellowship is sweet, attendance is encouraging, and baptisms hit a recent high in 1994. Broadmoor Baptist Church is located at 3824 Austin Peay Highway.

C. Roy Stauffer, M.Div., D.Min., Senior Minister

Roy Stauffer received his Masters of Divinity and Doctorate of Ministry from The Divinity School at Vanderbilt University. During his years in seminary, he served churches in Nashville and western Kentucky.

Lindenwood Christian Church

Lindenwood Christian Church celebrated its 150th year as a congregation in 1993. The congregation is dedicated to proclaiming the good news of Jesus Christ in word and deed. In addition to strong ownership, music, education, children and youth ministries, the congregation is much involved in local and global missions. Lindenwood Christian Church is located at 40 East Parkway South.

Kenneth P. Story, M.Div., D.Min., Pastor

Ken Story was called to preach and licensed by Oaklawn Baptist Church in Kentucky when he was only 15. At 19, he began his first pastorate and was ordained by that same church. He went on to obtain a Bachelor of Arts from Union University as well as a Master of Divinity and a Doctorate inf Ministry from New Orleans Baptist Theological Seminary.

Germantown Baptist Church

Germantown Baptist Church has recently experienced

explosive growth as its membership increased from 200 to over 5,000 in the last three decades. The church is a body of believers committed to reaching their community for Christ. Germantown Baptist Church is located at 2216 Germantown Road South.

Kenneth Twigg Whalum, Senior Pastor

Kenneth Whalum, is a graduate of Booker T. Washington High School and LeMoyne-Owen College. He was president of the Tennessee Baptist Missionary and Educational Convention and State Vice President of the National Baptist Convention, USA, Inc. Since 1985, he has served on the Memphis City Council.

Olivet Baptist Church

Olivet Baptist Church was founded on August 15, 1924. Today, Olivet is one of the strongest Black Baptist churches in America, with an active membership of 1,500. Under God's direction and the leadership provided by the pastor, the church continues to move ahead with an awareness of its responsibilities to God and to the community. Olivet Baptist Church is located at 3084 Southern Avenue.

He will give
you strength to bear it.

He has given
us resources
and the
Available Way.
We can choose
the available
way, which
is usually
the harder,
less comfortable
and less compelling way.
Jesus lived it
and showed us.
The available
way is there every
hour, every minute.
It's the great gift that
spiritually allows us to be
most fully human, if we choose it.